One of the Queen's Horses

Also by Hazel Reed

Stage One Riding & Stable Management

Stage Two Riding & Stable Management and
The Riding & Road Safety Test

Stage Three Riding & Stable Management

The Preliminary Teaching Test

One of the Queen's Horses

Hazel Elizabeth Reed

Nova Publications

I DEDICATE THIS BOOK

TO

HER MAJESTY QUEEN ELIZABETH II

FOR THE CELEBRATION OF HER GOLDEN JUBILEE

MAY 2002

SHE INSPIRES US ALL.

Acknowledgements

There is so much help and assistance that goes into the making of a book that it becomes impossible to mention everyone; otherwise this would be a tome of massive dimensions. I would like to thank everyone, for no matter how small a contribution, every bit becomes a part of the book.

I would like to make a special mention to Sophie Reed, my daughter, without whom none of this would have been possible, her support was vital. To Helena Reed, my youngest daughter also for her assistance during the week and to Martyn my son who, through his quiet support and love, gives me so much encouragement. To Derek, who helps in so many ways, supporting and urging me onwards; sometimes being Devil's Advocate is an uncomfortable part. To Robert Pickles FBHS without whose guidance and teaching I would never have reached the standard I needed. To all the proofreaders, without them it could be gobbledegook.

A special mention to all the grooms who aided and supported the riders through that week; they were the unsung heroes of 'All the Queen's Horses'. To Jennie Loriston-Clarke for generously giving her time, energy and expertise to create something amazing. To Jane Bredin who quietly supported us all in the background and to all those riders who encouraged both Eeyore and me to do what we did, to rise above it all!

I wish to thank all the horses and ponies who throughout my life have shown such infinite patience in teaching me horsemastership. Lastly of course, thanks and special titbits to Eeyore II, a truly magnificent spirit, whose patience, forbearance, generosity of soul and whose love teaches me all the time. Every time I ride him I learn something new about myself. Without you Eeyore, nothing would be possible.

To Martyn, who wishes that:

'One of the Queen's Horses'

is also known as

'The Adventures of Mr. E.!'

Prologue

To celebrate the Golden Jubilee of our Queen, Elizabeth II, an extraordinary equine extravaganza was organised. This occasion, called 'All the Queens Horses', was performed at Windsor on the evenings of May 16th, 17th and 18th 2002. It brought together over a thousand horses and ponies, with two thousand riders, grooms and supporters for one memorable week in which the participants rehearsed and performed their set 'Acts' in front of the Royal Family.

As well as commemorating a unique event in our lives, that of the 50th year of the reign of our Queen, this event also thrillingly entertained thousands, possibly millions, through the performances and media coverage. The atmosphere of those performances, the excitement of the action and the pageantry captured the hearts of both horse lovers and of those who cannot comprehend the obsession that we have about horses and ponies.

Spectacular as the evening shows were, the greater story was hidden behind the scenes. The event created an environment filled with drama, emotional upheavals and some nerve-wracking moments between riders and their horses. In many cases the 'Acts' had to be learnt in just a few days, the horses and ponies acclimatized to the noise, smells and strange lights of the Stadium in a few hours. Within one week thousands of horses, ponies and humans had to learn, rehearse and perform some amazing feats of horsemanship; it strained relationships and took some to the very edge of their abilities.

This is a personal view of that week related by one rider who was fortunate to perform in this unique occasion. It is an amazing revelation through one week in the life of a participant, who had to push herself beyond the point of physical endurance, stretch the relationship between her and her horse to the limit and who, through determination and the love of her equine partner, won through to be a part of this momentous event.

This story too encapsulates all that is loveable about horses, their characters and personalities, their huge hearts, their giving and generous natures, their idiosyncrasies, their unpredictability and their sheer love of mischief. It demonstrates how close the relationship becomes between a rider and her horse, how strong the bond and how poignant the love can be between these two living creatures.

11

The Decision and its Future

Life has a way of throwing us challenges. It is up to us whether or not we accept these challenges and whether or not we see them through. It is not wrong to refuse, nor is it wrong to give up or fail. Sometimes though, we do need to pass through that hoop of fire, cross over that threshold of pain, to achieve the prize, to really discover more about ourselves and to live life to its fullest.

It was one of those challenges that was tossed my way when a friend stated that she was going to Windsor to be a part of the grand event 'All the Queen's Horses'. She explained about staying the week at Windsor with her horse and eventually riding in front of the Queen as part of the Jubilee Celebrations. I decided immediately to be a part of it, come what may.

The British Dressage Magazine, a publication for members of the British Dressage Group, featured a small article describing the proposed event. Included in this article was a paragraph

Medium Dressage

Medium standard is, as the name implies, between the basic, starting level of Preliminary and the highest accolade of Grand Prix. Dressage is standardised by levels as in any amateur, semi-professional and professional sport.

The levels are decided by Dressage Tests, the basic being Preliminary where the horse is ridden around an arena in basic circles, turns and straight lines at the three main paces of walk, trot and canter. Novice standard comes next followed by Elementary, Medium, Advanced Medium, Advanced, Prix St. George, Intermediare I and II and then Grand Prix. Each level asks for a higher degree of ability from horse and rider, more difficult movements and paces.

A horse can change and alter his pace quite dramatically, for instance walk can either be collected, slow but full of energy, medium with longer strides, extended where the horse stretches his frame and lengthens his stride, and free walk on a long rein. Similarly, with the trot and canter which can be collected, working, medium and extended. The transitions or changes between these paces have to be balanced, forward and smooth.

A horse needs to be working at a fairly advanced standard to perform a collected pace. Working in a collected pace (or in 'collection' as it is also known) means that though the pace is slower, the horse should still be stepping with energy. To ask a horse to go slower is not enough. The horse will take smaller steps but he may also lose the energy and literally go slower. The horse needs to take smaller but higher steps, he needs to retain and look to have the desire to spring forwards.

The horse also needs to keep a constant rhythm in all the paces maintaining the 'beat' of the pace. The walk should be a four-time beat with each hoof touching the ground at separate times. In a good walk, especially with a free walk on a long rein, the horse should be stretching forwards through his back; his legs on the same side should make a 'V' when the hoof of the hind leg almost meets the hoof of the foreleg. Trot is two-time with the diagonal fore and hinds moving together. Canter is three-time, one foreleg, a diagonal pair (the other foreleg and the corresponding hind leg) and the last hind leg.

To maintain rhythm in the movements and to perform the paces with energy, particularly in the collected paces, the horse needs to be working correctly, using his body efficiently and with agility. He needs to be, as it is termed, 'stepping through from behind'.

A horse's 'engine' is in his hindquarters, it is from there that his power comes; he needs to work from his hindquarters to push through this power to his forehand. For this he needs to be physically fit, having developed the right muscles, and he needs to be obedient to the rider. It is the rider who asks for the paces and the transitions and the horse needs to be responsive and obedient if the partnership is to work in harmony.

requesting riders to volunteer to be a part of this Equestrian Extravaganza in the dressage phase of this show.   Riders and horses had to be of medium standard to apply.   At medium dressage level a horse and rider need the ability to work in collected, working, medium and extended paces, that is walk, trot and canter.

Dressage is more complicated and subtle than it appears but as with every sport, once you know what you are looking for and understand the logistics, dressage becomes riveting, an absolute obsession. It is so subtle. The horse changes paces and varies his movements so slightly to such tiny signals from the rider that it is fascinating to observe.

Even without a vast knowledge of horses or dressage, to watch a horse and rider perform so gracefully, so effortlessly is just a delight in itself.   Learning about dressage and becoming experienced heightens the wonder and love of this sport. It is the true combining of two living creatures; nothing on earth touches it. Show jumpers, eventers, racing jockeys all need a rapport with their horses but in any sphere of equestrianism, it is the flat work, the schooling, the 'dressage' of riding, that is the basis of any success.

Look for the horse with power in his hindquarters; watch how he uses that power to energize the forward movement throughout his body. His hocks, the bend in the hind legs, should flex and flow, the shoulders and forehand should appear light and free moving.

I am a relative newcomer to dressage, though all my life it has fascinated and captivated me. How the rider develops a sufficient rapport with a horse that the horse performs certain movements, changes of pace, even going sideways and backwards at designated points in a dressage arena, is nothing short of miraculous.

Even more enthralling is dressage to music! Watching those horses moving to music is to be transported out of this world. It is not just dancing, though the horse seems to be doing ballet, it is the complete oneness between horse and rider, how the rider almost thinks the movement and the horse responds. Aah, the times I have sat and watched, and hoped, and fantasised!

And that is all it was, fantasy, watching and wishing. Until my chance came; I found the horse of my dreams, a jet-black 16 hand 1 inch high Hanoverian, a dressage horse working at Prix St. George level.

When I first saw him my jaw dropped; never in my wildest imagination did I think I would own such an incredibly beautiful animal. When he moved he floated. His feet never seemed to touch the ground; he glided on invisible wings. Both I, and my daughter Sophie, who went to view him, gasped with awe.

I took my chance (and the challenge that life tossed me at that point) and bought him as a schoolmaster. He has taught me more than I could ever have hoped, improving my riding ability beyond recognition. His name is Eeyore II.

I do not know the reason for this strange name. His sire, World Cup I, has progeny whose names all begin with 'W'. Eeyore's name was originally 'Watch Out' when he was brought over from Germany and, as it is unlucky to change a horse's name, it is strange that such an amazingly handsome horse was given such an odd name. It is true his ears may seem over large to some, but I think they are just right.

So, as the British Dressage Magazine article requested, Eeyore and I being at least of medium standard, I applied for a part in 'All the Queen's Horses' by sending our details to Jennie Loriston-Clarke for acceptance.

Jennie Loriston-Clarke is one of the top riders in the United Kingdom. She has won an impressive list of honours and prizes and is one of those names revered throughout the equine world. She is also a daunting personality, being strict, demanding and fastidious about correct riding. These traits are necessary to rise to the top in the dressage world as Jennie Loriston-Clarke has done, but it makes it fearful for all of us far below her standard! She is also one of my life's heroes. This was a challenge to start with, would I be of an acceptable standard for her?

Once I had faxed the relevant details, I then waited anxiously for the reply.

2

The Reply

The answer to my fax came some days later. A large brown package was pushed through the letterbox; the letter inside was headed with the gold and light blue emblem of 'All the Queen's Horses'.

It stated that the committee of 'All the Queen's Horses' would like to welcome me to the largest ever horse extravaganza. I had been accepted. I screamed and my family looked up from their breakfast in surprise.

'I'm in, I'm in,' I shouted. Had I known then what it entailed….no I would still have desired to go. To ride in front of the Queen, what a privilege, what an honour; I could not have missed it.

The letter continued to detail the commitment to this occasion:

Your Act is: **Balmoral**

Your Participation is: **Dressage**

Number of horses: **1**

Maximum number of personnel permitted: **2 per horse**

Costumes & Props: **to provide own Black jacket, breeches, black boots, black velvet hat**

'Ooh does that mean that I can be your groom?' squeaked twelve-year-old Helena, my youngest.

'What?' I looked at her eager, bright face.

'It says two people allowed per horse,' she insisted.

Despite the competition to be my groom, I chose my eldest daughter Sophie for various reasons, the most pressing being that she, at nineteen, is more capable of looking after herself. I, quite correctly, expected there to be times when I would be leaving Sophie on her own. A slight twelve year old in amongst a large number of horses would have been a worry. Disappointed as she was, Helena put on a brave face.

Enclosed with the letter was a huge pack of papers. These contained information on arrival times, rehearsal times, the documentation required and a map of the stables at Frogmore Barracks.

Frogmore is adjacent to Windsor and, though there are stables for horses at Windsor, the accommodation there is mainly for those competing in the Show itself. Windsor Horse Show is held for four to five days in mid-May and includes competitions for show jumping, showing, dressage and carriage driving.

As there will be too many horses and ponies partaking in the evening Celebration to be stabled at Windsor, participants for the evening extravaganza will be accommodated at Frogmore Barracks, which sounds rather posh.

Receiving the paperwork was the first step on our adventure. It was early April 2002, six weeks to go.

There are certain points in life where everything comes together, as though that point is the pivot of everything that has gone before. Just as all roads are reputed to lead to Rome, so every action, thought, every bend in the road of life leads to one particular event in time. This is exactly how I felt now.

If I had not purchased Eeyore, I would not have been able to apply for this occasion. If I had not heard that he was for sale and managed to find the money to buy him, life would have been very different.

If the conversation with my friend had not occurred, I would never have known about Windsor. If I had not belonged to the Dressage Group, I would never have found the piece in that magazine and so on, right through. It is at these times that life fulfils itself.

Life's pattern for one brief moment seems to make sense, aligns itself in one place. As though some hidden, divine, omnipotent hand just for an instant is visible, manipulating life, guiding it to its destination. Life seems full of coincidences, yet those coincidences appear to be planned, organised, as if Destiny shows its face from behind the veil of obscurity, just for a breath, then it is gone.

From the moment I received the acceptance, the important task was to keep Eeyore sound, making sure that he did not become injured, lame, wounded or ill. The next six weeks were anxious times. Eeyore needed to maintain his routine, working in the same way. He needed to go out to grass with other horses every day, but at any moment he could be kicked and wounded; step on a sharp object and suffer a puncture wound in his foot. Life

The Royal Mews

Owned by the Queen and situated next to Buckingham Palace, the Royal Mews is an historic place, having been in its present location since 1760 when George III moved his collection of horses and carriages from near Charing Cross. Over 100 coaches and carriages including those used by the Queen for state occasions are still kept here.

A few of the more notable ones include the Irish State Coach built in 1851 used by the Queen for the State Opening of Parliament. The Scottish State Coach, built in 1830, used for royal processions. Queen Alexandra's State Coach used to carry the Imperial State Crown to Parliament for the State Opening and the State Landau built in 1902 used for royal processions and occasions.

The Australians, to mark the Bicentenary, in 1988 presented the Queen with the Australian State coach and there is even a Glass coach built in 1881 used for royal weddings. The oldest Coach housed at the Royal Mews is the Gold State Coach.

It is an amazing sight on most early mornings to see the Queen's own small brougham, a one horse closed carriage, travelling around the streets of London transporting the Queen's messenger between the Royal residences.

As well as the vehicles, more than thirty horses are stabled and trained at the Royal Mews in preparation for their royal duties. The Cleveland Bays are middleweight horses originating from the part of the country after which they are named. True bay in colour, they have the brown body with black 'points', i.e. legs, mane and tail. Not to be confused with the 'brown' horse that is brown all over with no black points, or the strangely named 'liver' chestnut, which is a muddy coloured brown. Chestnuts of course, can vary in colour from what is sometimes termed the 'tomato soup' red, to a vivid auburn. Chestnut mares are reputed to be bad tempered though not all follow this unfortunate trait.

The Windsor Grey horses vary in colour, as do all grey horses. Some are almost a pure white (the only true white though is albino with pink eyes, extremely rare). Greys are called greys because no matter how white their hair, their skin underneath is dark. Dapple-greys are popular; the marbled effect of their coat can be attractive, whereas the horribly named 'flea-bitten' greys have tiny spots and marks. Iron greys are almost a grey-black; some have lighter manes and tails.

As well as the greys and bays, the Queen owns horses of other colours such as the beautifully marked skewbalds with brown and white patches. Just as attractive the handsome piebald is black and white, and the rare multi-coloured is a mixture of brown, black and white.

Horses come in an amazing variety of colours from golden Palominos to what must be the most unusual colour of all, Appaloosas. Horses of this colour are normally grey (white) with black spots, similar to a Dalmatian dog, but they can be mixtures of brown or bay, with white areas on which are spots or patches.

seemed full of accidents waiting to happen and he was watched carefully every single day.

During that time too, we had some preparation to do. Our 'Act' in the show was to be based on a Scottish theme. The information was that there would be loud bagpipe music from a bagpipe band, together with drums and Scottish dancers performing reels. I imagined a six-foot highland Scot in full dress uniform, kilt and all, standing in front of Eeyore with a huge set of bagpipes across his shoulder. Acclimatisation time.

Playing loud music whilst schooling Eeyore in the 20 x 40 metre school at our yard happens only occasionally. From now though, he will be subjected to loud bagpipe music every time he works.

We play music on the ghetto blaster by the massed bands of the Argyle and Sutherland Highlanders and the Gordon Highlanders. Eeyore does not turn a hair. He is not even anxious by my walking around with a spade over my shoulder imitating a bagpiper. He just looks quizzically at me and appears to shrug his shoulders as if to say, there goes my Mum again!

Other acclimatising activities we use to prepare Eeyore during these weeks are flag waving, drum banging, rapping sticks on the fence, trumpeting sounds, cracks from leather whips, all of which he takes in his stride. Even Helena and me dancing Scottish reels in the school whilst Sophie rides him has no effect. We whirl and wheel, flaying our arms about, yelling, whooping and cheering. He is quite unconcerned; he seems bombproof.

It is quite usual to acclimatise horses with loud music and other strange activities. For instance, the horses who pull the Queen's coaches are subjected to loud music almost every day. The Windsor Greys and the special Cleveland Bay horses who live at the Royal Mews have the sounds of military bands and drums played at full volume so that they stay calm when performing at Royal occasions.

So Eeyore is acclimatised to music and drums. In the weeks leading up to Windsor, we also begin to titivate his body. He has several baths when the weather is sufficiently warm and Sophie frequently practises plaiting his mane and tail. His tack and clothing are cleaned thoroughly; we even clean the grooming kit.

Though Eeyore has been shod more recently than the six weeks when horses normally need shoeing, the blacksmith is called in to fit him with new shoes. I do not want him to have a loose shoe, to completely shed or 'cast' a shoe both of which could cause him to go lame. I am sure there will be a blacksmith at Windsor for any emergencies but I would prefer to avoid any problems.

Those few weeks go by slowly and quickly, the elasticity of time. It seems an age since being accepted yet there does not seem time to do everything. Inevitably, April goes, a beautiful sunny, dry April and May enters, colder and slightly wetter. Soon we approach the Day of Departure.

3

Saturday 11th May
24 Hours to go

Preparation – anxiety – self-doubt – reluctance – nerves and irritability

There, outside our house is the horsebox. We need to clean and prepare it for Sophie and I who are going to stay in it for a week. I, who hate camping, whose idea of holidaying is a three star hotel (or better still a four star) with facilities, am going to stay in a horsebox!

The box is not new; it does look a bit battered around the edges but I am proud of it. It is the first horsebox I have owned and now that it has two new batteries, a new ramp and a repaired exhaust, it does its job well.

The living space inside has an oven, hob, grill, fridge and cupboards. There is room for two to sleep over the cab in the mysteriously named 'luton' and room for another two by removing the table and putting the boards down in the 'lounge' area. It will be like staying in a doll's house. There is also a shower room complete with shower and a rudimentary toilet, one of those chemical boxes which none of us knows how to use. I am hoping that the toilets at Frogmore will be easily available on site but should we need a toilet during the night, there is at least this one.

Preparations include gathering together the bedding, food, cooking utensils, horsey gear, first aid kits, hot water bottles, bottles of water to drink, horse feed and hay. Keeping busy is essential because the moment I stop the sickness starts; my stomach has been queasy for some days and there is a slightly faint coppery taste in my mouth.

During those moments of rest, anxieties creep in, feelings of not being good enough, lack of confidence in myself. Should I be doing this; riding a dressage drill with other riders and horses in front of Her Majesty the Queen, Prince Philip, the Princess Royal, the Earl and Countess of Wessex and other members of the Royal Family, under the auspices of Jennie Loriston-Clarke? Continue working, it is the best remedy for nerves.

There was a slight hiccup a few days before departure and again, it was just one of those coincidences that saved the day. I belong to the local Riding Club dressage team scheduled to ride in the Rural Riders Qualifier at Newbury Show on May 26th, a week after 'All the Queens Horses'. To enter many competitions and events it is compulsory that horses have a full vaccination certificate.

Horses are inoculated annually against such diseases as equine flu and tetanus. When I bought Eeyore though, for some unfathomable reason, his vaccination programme had lapsed, he was not covered. To start, or restart, a vaccination programme the horse has an initial inoculation, followed no less than 21 days and no more than 90 days by a secondary inoculation and six months later by a third booster, after which annual boosters are given. The Vet has to note on a certificate, the date of the inoculation, the type of drug used and validate it with an official stamp of the Vet's name and address.

A complete vaccination certificate shows all inoculations, including the initial ones, together with details of the horse, so that certificates cannot be used by anyone else. Eeyore was given his initial and remaining set of inoculations after I purchased him in November 1998.

On the Thursday evening prior to the Sunday departure to Windsor, a meeting was arranged with the organiser of the team dressage when she checked that Eeyore's vaccination certificate was up to date. She immediately noticed that there was no record of his initial or secondary inoculation on his certificate. Eeyore's certificate only showed his first annual inoculation and the subsequent ones afterwards.

Then I remembered that he had been given a new certificate because the dogs at the stable where I kept Eeyore at the time had chewed his original one. When the Vet had written out a new certificate, the original details were not transferred.

That was problem enough for the team dressage at the end of May. For Windsor in two days it was worse, the authorities at Frogmore were insisting on having a full inoculation record for each horse, from the initial vaccination onwards.

If we could not discover the Vet and obtain a copy of the original inoculations, we would not be allowed into Frogmore. After three years and two stables ago, how could the original vaccinations, or a copy of the originals, be obtained? I needed to ring the Vet whose stamp was on the first annual vaccination in autumn 1999.

Would they have a record of Eeyore II? Would they have a record of giving the initial and secondary vaccinations? If their Veterinary Practice had not done the inoculations, it would be serious. I could not recall which other Vet it could have been.

'Hold on' was the answer on the telephone and there was silence, apart from my heart, which was pounding. Had they a record of Eeyore? Time went by slowly. Then a voice uttered, 'Let's see.'

More time and silence, I secretly prayed. Then the lady stated 'Yes, we have a record of Eeyore II.' But was this the Vet who inoculated him? Another silence as she searched through the records. If the answer is no, I am stumped.

'Yes we have a record of both initial and secondary vacs.' Huge sigh of relief. All that was required now was to obtain a record of these vaccinations. There was no time for posting, it would mean driving the two hours there and back for the stamped certificate. My husband Derek jumped to the rescue.

That was close. Had it not been for that team dressage, Windsor may not have happened for us. A thorough check was made through all the Windsor information for any further documents required.

The only worry now, will Eeyore be able to face the music, literally?

Horses are seemingly unpredictable creatures. Sometimes they will 'spook', back off or even bolt at top speed, at any tiny thing. A leaf out of place, a strange coloured fence, a plastic bag blowing in the wind, these are enough to set a horse galloping in the other direction. On occasions though they can ignore the loudest noises, the brightest lights, it all depends on how they see their world around them.

In their natural environment, horses are prey. They are hunted as food by packs of wolves, mountain lions and even humans, who can be predators at times. Horses have developed their instincts accordingly. Their eyes, positioned on the side of the head, have an almost all round peripheral view. They see things behind them we cannot see. Their senses are tuned to catching scents of predators, to hearing sounds, such as quiet rustlings as something stalks them. Horses are often more afraid of crouching plastic bags in corners than of huge tractors with extending arms because the bags imitate a waiting predator in ambush, the tractor is a massive object out in the open.

Horses are contrary creatures; a horse will spook at something one day and not the next. That is what makes horses so exciting and absorbing, not much time for thinking of other worries and problems when riding a horse!

Even for experienced equestrians, horses can be an unfathomable mystery and at times totally unpredictable. For instance, all through our acclimatisation period, Eeyore was not affected by the loud bagpipe music played on a ghetto blaster or by us whirling like dervishes around the school. Yet, when I attempted to hand to my daughter Sophie, who was riding him at the time, a small plastic bottle of water for her to drink from, Eeyore shot across the arena at the speed of light!

Horses! There is just no knowing what they will do next.

4

Sunday 12th May
Day 1

This is it! Excitement – nervousness – anticipation – disillusionment

Rising at 6 a.m., we put the last few necessities in the box. We prepare Eeyore for travelling, putting on his travel boots to protect his legs, (horses can injure themselves quite severely being rocked around in a horsebox) the tail bandage to protect his tail against rubbing and a summer rug to keep him warm without heating him. Finally we depart the stables and begin our journey to Windsor.

Security seems tight at Frogmore so only Sophie and I are going; we are not sure that others in the family will be allowed entrance. I am driving the horsebox, which I enjoy; it gives me the feeling of being on equal terms with all those other great lorries on the road. As a precaution, because I am notorious for losing my way, we have already driven over to Frogmore the previous weekend, so I know what to do at all the roundabouts and where the Shaw Gate entrance is situated.

The drive takes about an hour and, by the time we arrive at the entrance gate, my heart is pounding; this is reality, it is no longer a dream, an imagined future.

The 'Stop Barrier' is down, the gatekeeper sees that we are displaying the Frogmore Entry Sign in the window of the box.

'What group are you with?' he asks.

'Dressage.' I reply.

'Turn right here, then down the road and right again and immediately right again. They will direct you from there.'

The road is quiet at present, not too many horseboxes around. We reach a pitted stony lane bordered by a brown, ancient looking wall covered with climbing roses. At the end of the lane, in front of us, is a huge field in the middle of which are rows of wooden stables - temporary stabling – over three hundred wooden boxes planted on an open field. Where are the brick built barrack stables I have been boasting about?

'There'll be temporary stables,' Gemma, my livery yard owner, told me. 'Small wooden boxes, 10 by 10 feet with a canvas roof.' She smiled wickedly.

'Oh no,' I retorted full of confidence, 'not for the Queen's horses, they are stabling us at Frogmore Barracks. There will be proper stables.'

Perhaps I have too vivid an imagination but I had envisaged Georgian brick built stables, white washed walls and oak doors, proper metal hayracks, automatic waterers and a covered walkway in front of the stables so we would not get wet if it rained. Serves me right for boasting!

We drive into another field to our right where a dozen or so horseboxes are already parked. Sophie goes to find the Stable Management Office to obtain our stable number whilst I unload Eeyore. He starts to come down the ramp from the box slowly and then he sees the grass! Clover rich grass, the best there is, and a whole field of it. He bounds down the rest of the ramp headfirst. Before his hind legs touch the ground, he dives, mouth open, into that luscious grass. He thinks he has arrived in Heaven!

Sophie returns with Eeyore's number, 569, and as soon as we remove his travel boots and tail bandage, we attempt to lead him to his allocated stable. The grass here though is so tempting that it is only after several grass stops and mouthfuls later that we arrive at his wooden mid-terrace stable.

He is slightly cautious of the flapping canvas roof and the narrow door entrance. Then he sees what is growing on the floor of his stable, clover rich grass! He shoots into the stable and down goes his head again to eat his stable space. Sometimes he forgets he is a dressage horse, he thinks he is a pony!

The temporary stables, though smaller than Eeyore is used to, do prove adequate, even cosy and neighbourly with the other horses just a small wooden wall apart.

We leave Eeyore eating his floor and return to the Stable Management office to ask about shavings for the bedding (when he finally eats all the grass) and food for his mealtimes.

No shavings. No food!

Shavings have come and gone; more are on the way.

Food has come and gone; more is on its way.

The rumours start. Almost immediately a person in a stable near to Eeyore's tells us that the horses are allowed only two bales of shavings each for the week! In normal circumstances, horses can use two to three bales a week and that is for a bed already established. It could take an initial three bales just to start

Eeyore's bed and give him a deep enough surface. The stables are built directly on the ground which, though grass now, will quickly deteriorate to mud through the action of heavy metal shod feet.

Eeyore needs a bed of soft shavings because he will remain in this stable for more than twenty hours each day. If the ground remains hard his joints could suffer from the hours of standing. If the weather turns wet and the ground becomes churned up by the effect of metal shod feet he may slip and fall. At the very least standing on soft wet mud could give him thrush in his feet, a bacterial infection caused by wet muddy ground. He will also need to lie down at some time and lying down on mud may stain his coat.

Thankfully, Eeyore is black, which does have its advantages. It is the grey horses who stain easily. Grass stains are horrendous to remove from a grey horse, as are mud stains and stable stains. Greys can be beautiful to look at but a real nightmare to keep clean.

More worrying is the food problem. Though Eeyore will eat the grass quite happily this will not keep him fit and healthy. Especially not with the amount of work he will be doing. He needs supplementary feeding to maintain his energy, his physical stamina and weight. Grass, whilst it is the natural diet for a horse, only gives sufficient nutrients for maintenance, that is to maintain the bodily health and weight on light work or no work at all. For what Eeyore does, (dressage is a highly energetic exercise) he needs more nutrients, extra proteins, vitamins, minerals, just as an athlete needs extra nutrients to maintain muscle tone and energy.

Luckily, I have put a bag of horse cubes, a mixture of nutrients made into a solid pellet form, in the lorry and, though these are the higher energy type cubes containing extra nutrients, one bag will not last more than a few days.

Thankfully, the food did arrive later in the evening and we were able to obtain a bag of Mix, a processed mixture of foods such as oats, barley, cubes, vitamins and minerals, in appearance rather like muesli. As with horse cubes, mix is available in various nutritional levels, from convalescence mix for horses out of work through illness or injury, pasture mix for horses on light work, to the competition mix that Eeyore needs to keep him fit and healthy doing hard work.

Hay is available and there seems no shortage of this. We have brought Horseage, that sweet smelling and tasting alternative to hay, made from grass allowed to partially ferment and vacuumed packed before it is completely dry. It is higher in nutrients than hay.

We feed this to Eeyore to prevent any respiratory problems. Before I bought him Eeyore had suffered a chest infection. Horses can suffer from respiratory conditions such as hay fever, asthma, chest and lung infections. Dry hay can contain pollen, dust or ears of corn that aggravate respiratory problems. Horseage being moist and free from dust is excellent for horses with any type of respiratory difficulties.

Another way to help prevent respiratory problems is to feed damp hay. Soaking hay for at least 20 minutes in water dampens down the dust and makes the spores swell so that they do not lodge in the respiratory tubes.

Providing damp hay here at Frogmore though could prove a problem. The water taps, mounted on blue wooden posts, are some distance from the boxes. Damping down hay and carrying a heavy wet haynet across a hundred yards or so is not feasible, at least not without a wheelbarrow. Those people who had obviously spent time at competitions and similar events had the foresight to bring a wheelbarrow. This item I will take to events in the future. We live and we learn.

We have not brought sufficient Horseage for the week so we decide to give Eeyore half Horseage and half dry hay. The hay available is fortunately of good quality and Eeyore is quite happy to eat it.

The water taps do cause work; Eeyore will need around 8 gallons of water every day. If the weather turns hot or he sweats profusely, which he may do with hard work and stress, he will need up to 15 gallons.

Two or three times a day we will need to refill Eeyore's two buckets and carry them the hundred yards or so back to his stable. This is different from the automatic waterers in the boxes that I had imagined. Still, we are doing this for the Queen, so stop moaning. At least I will build my muscles up this week!!!

Tea is scheduled for 5.00 p.m., in the huge catering tent situated next to the toilets and showers. This is five minutes walk from our box, along the road in front of the stables and through an ornamental gateway. The food is wonderful. There are meat dishes and vegetarian dishes plus accompanying vegetables all piping hot; salads, bread rolls with butter, and puddings. Well done, the catering corps, you did us proud!

After tea, we manage to obtain two bags of shavings. Eeyore looks on in disgust as we lay down a bed in his stable, completely covering that excellent grass! We give him his tea and hay, clean out his water buckets and refill them. He looks content.

At 7.00 p.m., we are invited to the catering tent for a welcome speech. The tent is packed with people from the British Isles and all over the world.

To our right is the Pakistani cavalry with their beautiful green uniforms and fantastic large leather boots that cover their knees and part of the upper leg.

To our left are representatives of the Indian cavalry, not so colourful tonight as they are in ordinary suits. It is an irony that whilst the Pakistani and Indian cavalry are with us this week, performing together in front of the Queen, the relationship between their two countries deteriorates every day bringing them to the brink of war.

Around us in the tent are Canadian Mounties, Australian Jackeroos, Policemen from New York, members of the American Carriage Society, a detachment of the Mounted Police from Kenya, the French Garde Republicaine Cavalry and many others. There are members representing the Side-saddle Club, the Arab Society, the Dressage Group, the Scottish dancers, the Hunting community and the Carriage Society. So many people from every corner of the earth are here in this tent.

I am beginning to realise that this is something massive, something special that includes thousands and thousands of people, participants, grooms, supporters, organisers and production teams. This is going to be such a huge, stupendous, immense occasion. My heart fills with pride and comradeship. We are part of one gigantic whole, here to celebrate and honour our Queen. It is a tearful moment.

This sort of organisation has taken hundreds of people many, many months, even years to create, design and arrange. Even a perfect 'white' horse has been specially brought over from Germany to perform by rearing at the end of the show. I am overwhelmed to be a part, albeit a tiny part, in this massive event.

Especially when I learn that this is to be, in certain ways, reparation for the unfortunate cancellation of the Pageant of the Horse.

During 1997, this event was planned to celebrate the Queen and Prince Philip's Golden Wedding anniversary. Over 1,000 participants were to perform in Windsor Great Park. It took two years to plan; the riders and performers had been practising for months. I remember reading about it in the equestrian magazines; it did sound a spectacular event. It did not happen!

The weather was atrocious. It rained and rained and rained, all through May and June, and July was the wettest for over a century. The whole event had to be cancelled. The ground was awash with mud; no horse or pony, rider or handler could hope to perform in those conditions with safety. The disappointment was overwhelming.

The Pageant's committee decided then to start planning a celebration for the Queen's Golden Jubilee. Let's hope all will go well. Windsor has a weatherproof surface, thousands of pounds and hours of work has been spent on organising it, so that even in rain we should be able to ride safely on this ground.

There are so many people participating in this event, with their horses, ponies, carriages, carts as well as the riders, grooms and supporters.   As the welcome speech lists all the different nationalities, the excitement mounts, rising like a wave of pride and global comradeship.   There are people from all over the United Kingdom, from all around the Commonwealth and from so many different countries, nationalities, cultures; here to celebrate one event.   Each has their own national patriotism and it is heartening and breathtaking to know that from all corners of the world we can come together in peace as one people, mankind.

It is only on occasions like this that the barriers of politics and politicians, of rebels and revolutionaries are banished. We are one people celebrating a unique event. Yes, my heart did swell with joy, with hope and pride for us all.

Now all we need is that the horses and ponies will be able to cope with the unnatural and unusual surroundings, the sounds, the noises, the scents and the hundreds of other horses and ponies in the Stadium at the same time!

5)

Sunday 12th May
Day 1 Evening

Acclimatisation time

The first test will be tonight. We are scheduled to be at the Windsor Stadium 11.00 p.m., for an acclimatisation rehearsal. It will be dark; there will be shadows and strange noises. I have never ridden Eeyore at that time of night; horse riding is almost exclusively a daylight exercise.

Before we reach the Windsor Stadium, we have first to ride along the tracks through Frogmore Park. The public are not usually allowed in these areas; Frogmore is a private estate, part of the Home Park of Windsor Castle. The ride from Frogmore barracks to the Stadium constructed at Windsor will take us 45 minutes. We have no idea how massive the Stadium is or what sounds, lights and other disturbances we will discover there.

This will be a test for Eeyore and me. If Eeyore 'flips', if he shies, spooks, backs off, refuses to go in the arena, bucks, rears, or bolts off at a fast gallop, I will be dismissed; I will not be allowed to take part. That would be such a disappointment (an understatement) after all these weeks.

My heart is in my mouth. This is the big moment. Will those years spent gaining his trust come to fruition? Will he trust me sufficiently to go into a situation that is frightening, exciting, strange, threatening? Will he understand that I would not lead him into danger?

At 8.30 p.m., we start by tacking up the horses. There is a buzz of excitement in the air; most of us are feeling trepidation mixed with anticipation.

The whole of the dressage group will hack together from Frogmore to Windsor; the three quarter of an hour's ride is a good warm up for the horses before they arrive at the Stadium.

It is twilight when we depart, a time of strange shadows, half-light, half-dark, the most bewitching time of all. Bushes appear different; they take on mysterious shapes. Sounds echo in the still air, trees bow and creak like old men. Hay bales in a field take on the appearance of a pack of wolves; water babbling under a small bridge becomes the laugh of hyenas. There is a strange smell in the air born of stale daylight and fresh evening breezes. The dim light of the sky throws everything into silhouettes, even the cows in a field are threatening spectres and cause some of the horses to skitter away from the track.

Usually at this time, Eeyore is tucked up in his stable munching his hay. Now he has to have his saddle and bridle on and be ridden the three miles or so to a strange arena, and hacked back again.

The atmosphere amongst our group is charged and the horses sense this. Some of them trot, refusing to walk; their metal shod hooves strike sparks of fire from the tarmac track. There is a smell of smoke in the air, of deep dark earth, of lichen-covered walls and musty black hollows.

Riders speak in whispers, holding tightly to the reins. The sensitive horses pick up these emotions; they can tell by the tightness of their riders' muscles in seat and legs; they feel the tension through their riders' backs and hands.

The grooms follow us on their bicycles; no cars are allowed on these tracks. It is too far to walk and impossible to keep up with the horses on foot. We can hear the swish of rubber tyres on the damp tracks, the occasional squeal of badly oiled brakes. Riding as slowly as they are is much harder than riding quickly.

Those grooms have the hardest job and I often recall their fortitude, hard work, and unrewarding endeavours on our behalf. For us, hard work though it is, at least we have the adrenalin boost of each night's performance, the honour and pleasure of riding a horse.

It is difficult to see individual riders on their horses but I do join up with a couple and we talk about the event. One rider is part of the Grand Prix section so she is a competent rider. The other has taken part in similar events before so her horse is a seasoned campaigner. Yet, as she states, we are all in the same boat; there has never been anything organised on this scale previously.

We arrive at the River Thames. It is now total night. The colours are leached out of the landscape. The huge floodlights along the tracks only emphasise the contrast of black and white by making some areas very bright but leaving others extremely dark. The grass appears as a silver carpet, the tarmac road a grey ribbon, the river is a black moving snake marked with bright spots from the reflected lights.

The road into Windsor crosses over the river via Victoria Bridge. We riders and horses have to pass under this Bridge through a small tunnel next to the river. This tunnel is not lit; it is like entering a black hole. There is no apparent way through; it is a gaping cavern leading to unknown depths in the bowels of the earth.

The leading horses sniff and snort at the fearful maw in front of them, their eyes are peeled wide with trepidation and anxiety. The riders urge them on with firm leg aids and encouraging voices. Hesitatingly they begin to pass through but there is a sudden clatter of sound. It is the noise of their hooves on the cobblestones echoing around the stone arch. Now their suspicions are fulfilled. Some of the horses stop, arching their backs in fear, others twist around ready for flight but are blocked by the crowd at the tunnel entrance.

More and more horses begin to gather around the dark gaping hole. The cracking echoes from the total blackness are unfamiliar and feel dangerous. There is the scent of fear in the air, the sounds of horses desperately trying to escape some hidden horror. Some refuse to enter, backing up into others behind, causing them to stop and hesitate. Some rush through, starting with hesitant steps then bolting into the dark.

It does not help that the far side of the tunnel is barricaded with a barred gate; only the centre portion of this is open. It is just wide enough for two horses side by side to pass through. As horses speed through uncontrollably, clattering on the stones, some of the riders knock themselves against the bars of the barricade.

One horse rears up at the entrance and spins round. Another backs off refusing to enter the black archway. This causes a blockage of horses, bunching bodies, twisting and turning, dark eyes surrounded by white fear. Muscles bulge, sinews tighten, fear lends the horses strength, makes them disobedient. Panic is only a hair's breadth away as the fear spreads like an infection through the herd.   I am only too conscious of the deep, flowing river behind us, down a slippery slope of grass.

Eeyore stares with frightened eyes at the melee of horses; I talk to him gently, stroking his neck.   One horse passes us and trots across the cobblestones.   I gently nudge Eeyore with my legs to make use of this horse's slipstream.   Horses are often braver if following another; the herd instinct takes over.

It works, he goes in, but the noise of his hooves clattering in the small stone chamber frightens him, he throws his head up, his neck spasms into steel bands, his mouth is hard and unyielding.   I urge him on; we dare not stop.   He speeds on through the open gate, exiting the other end like a cork from a champagne bottle. We are safe!

Beyond the bridge, we turn to the left and up a small incline. Feeling the grass beneath his feet again and out in the open air; Eeyore relaxes.   It is lighter here too; the road to our left that goes over the bridge has streetlights and in front of us we can see, for the first time, the huge spotlights shining on top of massive scaffolding around the Stadium.

We continue to walk around the Windsor show ground; so different at this time of night.   The silver velvet grass is punctuated with small puddles left by the showers that day, they appear as reflective holes in the ground.

As we approach the Stadium, we can see a structure built high, a massive backdrop, brightly coloured.   There are bright lights and loud music emanating from this structure.   All the horses prick up their ears; bright eyes look at the strange surroundings, their nostrils dilate as they sniff the scents on the wind.   Some snort with excitement, blowing puffs of hot, misted breath into the cold night air.

They toss their heads and pick up their feet; gather their strength in their hindquarters.   I feel Eeyore's muscles bunch beneath me, yet he is not afraid, not as he was under that bridge.   What I feel is

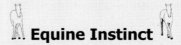

Equine Instinct

Horses will detect even the slightest tension. Because their lives are dependent on their senses, these are finely tuned. Their sight, hearing and sense of smell are far greater than ours. Their skin is prickled with nerve endings and their muscles ready for flight in an instant.

We as predators, (though we can also be prey), do not fully understand their super sensitivity and the instinct necessary for survival.

We do however use these instincts to help us train, ride and work these wonderful creatures. As when I utilised the herd instinct to manoeuvre Eeyore through the bridge.

Horses are herd animals; it is safer to live in large numbers, less likely to be picked out as a kill. A horse will often follow another into a strange place, a place he would refuse to go on his own.

Another part of the herd instinct is that the herd has a dominant individual, usually the top stallion, who keeps watch and warns the herd of danger. He must be obeyed without question; democracy is not a tool for survival as prey. The decision to run has to be made instantly.

We, as riders, need to be the head of the herd. To achieve this we need to gain the horse's trust. We need the horse to trust us sufficiently that he will follow our lead, and accept our demands without question.

To gain this trust we need his respect; that comes from being dominant but not bullying. Bullying creates fear and, in time, fear turns to revolution. We need dominance with love; we need respect with trust.

It is a fine balance achieved through discipline, not only for the horse, but also self-discipline for the rider. It is then that horses will often perform the most amazing actions required by the rider or handler.

As an integral part of this dominant bond, horses sense the slightest worry, hesitation and doubt on the rider's part. We need to keep patient, calm and confident if our horses are to remain calm as well.

excitement, a tension born of anticipation. I quieten him with words and stroke him along his neck. He bends his neck and watches me with one eye, questioning silently as he does.

'It will be fine,' I assure him. 'I am with you, you need have no fear.'

He snorts once and nods his head as if replying in the affirmative.

We enter what will become known to us in the evenings ahead as 'the Chute'. This is a long passage about 20 feet wide. To our left is the main road into Windsor separated from us by a tall metal fence. On our right are metal barricades, behind which are marquees. We halt here, waiting to enter the Stadium from the 'wings'.

There is a strange silence as we wait in the half dark. In front of us by contrast, the Stadium is a bay full of light and sound. We are silent because we are experiencing a mixture of emotions; anxiety – what will the horses do in these strange surroundings; excitement - the atmosphere is electric; anticipation - what will we experience when we enter?

We are silent too because we are keeping as calm as possible so that the horses remain relaxed and quiet. Horses are telepathic and empathic; they sense the thoughts, feelings and emotions of their riders, having an awareness of their fears and anxieties.

If the 'predator' on their back is afraid, there must be something fearful around. We need to maintain calmness and relaxation, which is difficult when the muscles react in such subtle ways that even a human is sometimes unaware of the changes within his own body.

In the Chute, we wait silently, consciously relaxing the muscles in seat and thighs. I breathe deeply, blowing puffs of air through my mouth, taking in deep breaths through my nose; I can feel the excitement begin to knot in my stomach, make my head spin.

The only sounds are the occasional swish of a tail, the stamp of an impatient hoof, or the jangle of a metal bit as a horse tosses his head.

Suddenly it is our turn; the usher is waving us in and slowly we walk towards the entrance. We stride into the Stadium, stepping from the dark passage of the Chute into a bowl of light and sound.

To our right is a fence made up of material fillers, advertising something and flapping in the slight breeze. Eeyore bends his head and neck to the right to peer at these formidable threats. He steps to the left, preparing for flight. I put my left leg firmly on his side and bend his head slightly away from the fence. Give him something else to think about, keep his attention away from the 'proposed threat'. He looks around at the imposing space; sand covered floor, lights bouncing around, glaringly reflected off the backdrop.

The arena is half filled with horses, people, carriages and carts. It is so brightly lit that it hurts the eyes.

As we arrive at the front of the Stadium, there is a smattering of applause; Eeyore turns to face the audience. He is not frightened I can feel that, he is excited, lit up by the atmosphere.

The voice over the loudspeaker tells us to walk all the way along the front of the Stadium, then left towards the back. We finally fit into line by the side of some other horses waiting patiently.

The large, bay thoroughbred horse next to us is called Jinksy, his grandfather being the famous racehorse, Nijinksy. He is one of the 'Hunting Group'. At first Eeyore and Jinksy eye each other up, appraising each other. Jinksy is taller than Eeyore but being a thoroughbred is of slighter build. After looking each other up and down, they snort quietly once and ignore each other.

We wait patiently as more and more horses, ponies, carts and carriages, riders and handlers enter the Stadium. The horses and ponies are all shapes, sizes, colours and breeds.

In front of our line is the mounted division of a constabulary with their colourful black and reflective yellow uniform. There are mounted policemen here from every division in the United Kingdom. They come from the Metropolitan Police, Avon & Somerset, City of London Police, Cleveland Constabulary, Greater Manchester, Humberside, Lancashire, Lothian & Borders Police, Merseyside, Northumbria, Royal Parks Police, Strathclyde, Thames Valley, South Yorkshire, West Yorkshire, Hull, Nottinghamshire and other regions. Amazing! I had no idea that the police still maintained so many mounted divisions with so many horses!

I look around, the Stadium is massive; I calculate approximately 150 metres wide by around 80 metres deep. The 'proscenium' the Lion and Unicorn arch in the background is around 15 metres high; it surrounds a space in the centre allowing room for the 75 piece orchestra and 150 voice choir. The music tonight is not as loud as it will be during the performances but it still feels almost as loud as a rock concert.

There are over a thousand lights lighting up the Stadium like midday, some from the massive structures either side of the Stadium that also house the T.V. cameras. In front of us are the seats for the audience, in the centre of which a section has been reserved solely for the Royal Family and their entourage.

The loudspeaker informs us that they are attempting to fit a thousand horses in here together with carriages, carts and drays. There is a little conversation 'offstage' and then the voice states that there are now seven hundred and fifty horses in this Stadium!

All those horses, all those incredible living animals, with their flicking ears, their widening nostrils, their nodding heads, their soft breathing flanks, their swishing tails and the occasional whinny answered by a neigh. All that horse flesh carrying riders, pulling carts and carriages, being led by hand; from the smallest about 11 hands high, (around 44 inches - 4 inches to a hand) to the largest Shires at 19 hands with their dinner plate feet. I have never seen so many horses and ponies together at one time.

Eeyore backs up but I send him forward to stand in line. He kicks his back leg out, which he normally does when he has a fly bothering him under his belly. There are no flies around tonight; he is becoming impatient. It is exciting in here and I feel myself shiver, at which point Eeyore backs up again and once more I have to persuade him to return to his spot.

More horses and ponies are being brought in now. Small Shetlands no larger than large dogs are being led in hand by the bridle or headcollar, or are pulling small carts. Coloured horses with their attractive multi-coloured coats, Palominos with their beautiful golden coloured bodies and silver-white manes and tails. Large Shire horses to pull the carts and drays. There are Polo ponies, racehorses, horses for side-saddle and hundreds of ponies from the pony clubs all around Britain.

The loud speaker then requests that the mounted Police in front us move off to the left. There is a momentary silence. The police look confused, helmeted heads move from side to side in Wimbledon fashion. Then discipline takes over and obeying orders they turn to their left, directly into the sides of some dressage riders standing quietly. There is consternation and a piled up queue of horses and riders going nowhere.

 'No, no,' shouts the loudspeaker voice, 'I mean to **your** right, my left. Lead out.'

There is some relieved laughter and the police turn their horses around towards the exit of the Stadium.

It is our time to depart; we turn to our right towards the Chute. Just as we approach the exit Eeyore sees a pony no bigger than a Great Dane, it appears to be completely white. Eeyore does not like that much, he steps to one side, his eyes out on stalks.

I breathe a sigh of relief as we make our way down the Chute and back onto the path for the hack home. We did it! We did it! We managed to stay in one piece, relatively quietly in that atmosphere, at this time of night.

On the way back to Frogmore Barracks, I physically relax. The return hack takes a different route, starting from Victoria Bridge and proceeding along the riverbank. Floodlit with strong white spotlights, this path seems brighter. Tall, slender trees border the track and a grass sward slopes down towards the Thames. Let us hope there are no problems here, because if a horse starts to back down that slope, both horse and rider will be in the river. I turn my head away; no thoughts like that tonight.

I am so happy. Eeyore was brilliant, he did not shy, he did not back up too much, he was totally controllable and quiet. Perhaps we may achieve this after all.

The riders and horses are not the only ones pleased and relieved. For the grooms, including dear, gallant Sophie, it has been a nervous and arduous time. They have cycled all the way between Frogmore and Windsor, determined to be there, on hand anywhere on the track, should their riders need them.

It will become a familiar sight in the evenings, groups of horses, punctuated by small bands of cyclists in support. It is an unforgettable memory those shadowy spectres on their bikes trailing us back and forth along the dark tracks. I know many of them suffered considerable aches and pains, but there were times when we were extremely glad of their help.

Eeyore and I reach Frogmore at 11.30 p.m. Sophie arrives on her bike just after us. We give Eeyore a small feed, fill his haynet, change his water and put on his rug. By this time, it is the other side of midnight.

Just as we finish our tasks, the lady in the stable next door informs us that we are expected at a practice tomorrow morning, mounted, at 8.30 a.m., with Jennie Loriston-Clarke. Need a good night's sleep then, this is the start of a tough road!

That night tucking ourselves into our beds, (Sophie scrambles up into the luton and I am on the 'bed' where the table usually is), we talk about our day. I am wound up from all the excitement and anxious about the riding tomorrow.

As a synopsis, I am slightly disappointed about the stables and the facilities. Temporary stabling with canvas roofs that flap and creak in the wind, no bedding on the floor just grass, and water taps a distance away. So much for posh boxes, food laid out in bins and automatic waterers!

Putting down the shavings for Eeyore's bed has made a difference though; the stable now seems quite cosy and I am sure we will manage the water between us. Then I recall all those people in the catering tent, from every corner of the world; it makes me realise how lucky and privileged I am to be here.

As for Eeyore, I was proud of him tonight; he was good in unfamiliar circumstances. I know he competed at a high level and is used to the applause and noise of competition, but he is also a highly-strung, physically fit animal, he could have taken it into his head to shy at anything. He did well.

The floodlight, that lights up the field where the horseboxes are parked, shines in through the window of the cab. Not that I mind, I cannot sleep in total darkness. There is a generator humming away, as it provides electricity to those boxes that have TV's, hot showers and plugs for hairdryers. About 1 a.m., I drift off to sleep. This is the start of a truly memorable week.

6

Monday 13th May
Day 2

Rain – rain – rain – mud and more mud. A cold, wet fiasco. It is the 13th!

At 7 a.m., Sophie and I rise to feed Eeyore. He seems to have settled into his temporary stabling.

As I have to ride him at 8.30, he needs his feed before 7.30. He cannot be ridden until an hour after his food. If ridden too soon his bulging stomach will press against his lungs and cause breathlessness, or he could suffer from colic, a potentially fatal condition of the digestive tract.

We give him some Mix with three handfuls of cubes, plus some of his additives. Like an athlete, he has extra supplements to maintain his body fitness. He has Cortaflex to keep his joints supple, a plop of Linseed oil, which helps to keep his coat shiny and hooves in good condition. He also has a product called Blue Chip Pro; this contains various vitamins and minerals and is excellent for keeping horses in good condition. He has a scoop of electrolytes, essential salts that can be lost through sweat. These are vital for the horse in hot weather, when he is doing hard work or when he sweats through stress or anxiety.

We fill his haynet with a mixture of hay and horseage, clean out and refill his water buckets. Then we walk over to the catering tent for breakfast and a wash.

At 8.15 a.m., we tack Eeyore up using his double bridle. This bridle has two metal bits that go into his mouth, instead of the single snaffle bridle that has one. Horses who have been trained to a higher standard are ridden using a double bridle as it offers a finer feel in the mouth and allows greater communication through more subtle use of the rider's hands. The rider does need to ride with a finer feel of the hands, for the double bridle can be severe if used in a strong, hard fashion.

The dressage group are to meet in a field behind the stables where, on the map sent to us prior to our arrival, are marked three rehearsal schools. Schools are areas measuring 20 metres wide by 40 or 60 metres in length; normally at Medium standard the school would be 60 metres long.

The three 'rehearsal arenas' I presumed would be of a sand or rubber surface, specially designed to provide a good work surface for horses. To my absolute amazement and horror, there are no schools at all! No, here is a field of newly cut grass with a great swathe of ploughed earth down the middle of it.

Where do we practise? On the grass and mud. There are no marked areas for schools, the field slopes slightly and the grass is wet from the morning dew.

The sky is a dull leaden grey promising more rain for later. I cannot believe it.

As I walk Eeyore into the field, I suddenly think how impossible this is going to be. Here are forty intermediate riders; most have never met prior to this week. We are hoping to ride a complicated arrangement of movements that we need to practise and make perfect in two days with horses of very different paces and abilities.

To put this into perspective, it usually takes me two to three weeks to learn an individual dressage test, lasting for four to five minutes. I spend hours practising each movement to ride it all correctly and this is a test I am performing on my own, no other horses involved.

Though in dressage competitions one single horse performs a previously learnt set of movements within an arena, there are times when more than one horse performs. On special occasions, two horses can perform a 'pas de deux'; four horses a quadrille and up to six or eight horses a drill ride. But it all takes time. Our riding club dressage team has spent the last three months practising its test with six riders, on a sand and rubber arena.

For this event, we are being divided into two groups; each group will consist of *twenty horses performing in one arena*. We will be riding one complicated test of six to seven minutes duration, including some quite skilled manoeuvres. We have to learn this routine within a few hours and perform it in front of the Royal Family and a live audience, in a stadium full of lights, sounds, other horses, carriages, dancers, pipes and drums!

My stomach turns over; what am I doing? There is no way this is going to work. If we had been practising this for weeks beforehand, had been able to join up with the other riders, had time to allow the horses to acclimatise to the extraordinary surroundings, then it would have been possible.

As a further challenge, the facility on which we are expected to do this is a grass and mud field. This is going to need some guts and skilful riding!

We start to walk around the field in pairs. I choose a lady I know on another Hanoverian horse, a liver chestnut; the friend incidentally who told me about this event. Eventually someone calls us over to gather in one large group in the centre of the field. There is Jennie Loriston-Clarke herself. She will need all her many skills if we are going to pull this off!

Jennie calls out our names and sends us to either Group 1 or Group 2. I am called up for Group 1 and am paired with another black horse, slightly smaller than Eeyore, a handsome Dutch horse.

We walk around in circles with our partners so that the horses can become accustomed to one another. Eeyore is a sociable gentleman who tends to mix with other horses. He pricks his ears once or twice at the horse beside him, whose name is Karim, sniffs his nose and then ignores him.

My partner and I chat about our horses and when I tell her that mine is called Eeyore II, she stops and peers at him.

Then her face lights up and she exclaims, 'I know him, I have seen him in competitions.' She looks at him with renewed respect. 'How did you get him?'

Eeyore is quite famous, wherever I go there is always someone who knows of him, has seen him somewhere. It never ceases to amaze me. I suppose because he is mine and familiar I do not think of him as being famous, it is only when someone recognises him that I realise how well known he is in the horsey world.

'You are so lucky to own him,' she states, 'he is extremely talented.' I know. He is teaching me!

It is a privilege to be instructed by Jennie Loriston-Clarke, who immediately begins licking us into shape with her sergeant major like orders. She chooses a piece of the field that is nearly flat; a piece that includes a ploughed up mud patch. At least this area is more suitable than the grassy slope, which is becoming slippery in the wet atmosphere.

It does mean though, that there are no markers from which to judge our movements.

Every dressage school or arena is marked out with letters all around the perimeter. The main letters are AKEHCMBF, which I believe originated from the French language. The mnemonic we use to remember them by is 'All King Edward's Horses Can Make or Manage Big Fences'. Other letters, D, G and X indicate spots on the centre line.

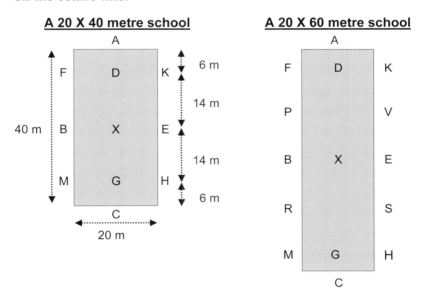

In dressage competitions, or when training and schooling the horse, these letters indicate the precise points for starting and finishing movements. For instance, in a 40 metre long arena, a 20 metre circle starting from A or C must go through X. At a higher standard the more difficult movements start from more difficult spots.

In larger arenas of 60 metres length there are even more letters, most of which I find difficult to remember!

A school is normally surrounded by a fence; an arena is marked out by white boards placed on the ground. The letters are placed around the perimeter. Those letters inside the school or arena have to be memorised.

To mark out the 'school' or 'arena' in this ploughed field, one lady positions herself approximately where 'A' would be and Jennie stands around 'C'. For the rest of the boundaries and letters we have to make calculated guesses. This sort of situation has the result of toughing one up!

We begin by walking through the whole routine, though all of the movements will be performed in trot and canter.

In pairs, we ride up the 'centre line', from A to C. We need to ride stirrup to stirrup with our partner. The sign of good pairs riding is the clinking of stirrups, when the stirrups of both riders touch. This shows that the pair is riding close together and in time, that one is not in front of or behind the other. We also need to be directly behind the pair ahead of us. The usual distance behind the pair in front is one horse's distance but with twenty riders in one arena this distance has to be decreased. We may end up riding nose to tail!

At the end of the centre line, at 'C', the pairs split. Following the horse in front we ride around the edge of the arena and do a movement called 'shoulder-in' down the long side.

In our routine for Windsor, once we complete the shoulder-in down the long side of the 'school' we straighten the horse and turn onto the short side, to pair up with our partner and ride down the centre line. From this line we now ride a ten metre circle, touching the 'outside' of the school, or 'track' as it is called, and back to the centre line.

The circle needs to be ten metres in diameter exactly and we need to ride this circle in time with our partner, to meet up on the centre line at precisely the same moment.

Shoulder In

The shoulder-in is such a beautiful movement to perform, having various benefits for both Eeyore and me. In this movement, the horse's shoulder is brought in at an angle of approximately 30° and he moves sideways, bringing one foreleg in front of and across the other, and one hindleg in front of and across the other. Keeping the angle constant, the horse moves on three tracks.

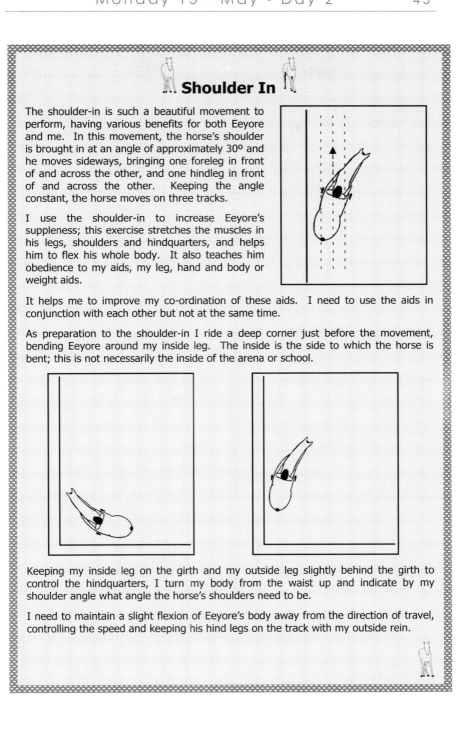

I use the shoulder-in to increase Eeyore's suppleness; this exercise stretches the muscles in his legs, shoulders and hindquarters, and helps him to flex his whole body. It also teaches him obedience to my aids, my leg, hand and body or weight aids.

It helps me to improve my co-ordination of these aids. I need to use the aids in conjunction with each other but not at the same time.

As preparation to the shoulder-in I ride a deep corner just before the movement, bending Eeyore around my inside leg. The inside is the side to which the horse is bent; this is not necessarily the inside of the arena or school.

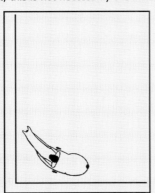
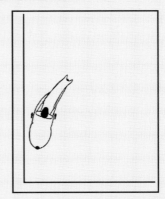

Keeping my inside leg on the girth and my outside leg slightly behind the girth to control the hindquarters, I turn my body from the waist up and indicate by my shoulder angle what angle the horse's shoulders need to be.

I need to maintain a slight flexion of Eeyore's body away from the direction of travel, controlling the speed and keeping his hind legs on the track with my outside rein.

It does help sometimes to start the shoulder-in from a circle. From a ten metre circle in the corner I reach the point on the circle where Eeyore's hind legs are still on the track but his shoulder is slightly in from the track and then, instead of completing the circle, I ask him to go sideways down the long side of the school.

Performing shoulder-in teaches me self-discipline for I need to maintain the angle throughout the movement whilst keeping Eeyore forward and active. Too great an angle and Eeyore will move on four tracks, (though in some countries this is correct shoulder-in), too small an angle and he will not bend his body but only his neck.

As with all movements in dressage the more Eeyore and I practise, the more we increase our rapport. At times I need only indicate by a slight movement of my shoulder and a miniscule touch of my legs and Eeyore does the shoulder-in. We reach a point almost when I think the movement and Eeyore responds. It is just so magic when a horse and rider becomes that close, two living beings thinking as one.

There is a movement similar to shoulder-in, which is called shoulder-fore. Here the horse's forehand is brought marginally in from the track.

For more advanced horses this movement can be used all the time because it maintains the horse's straightness.

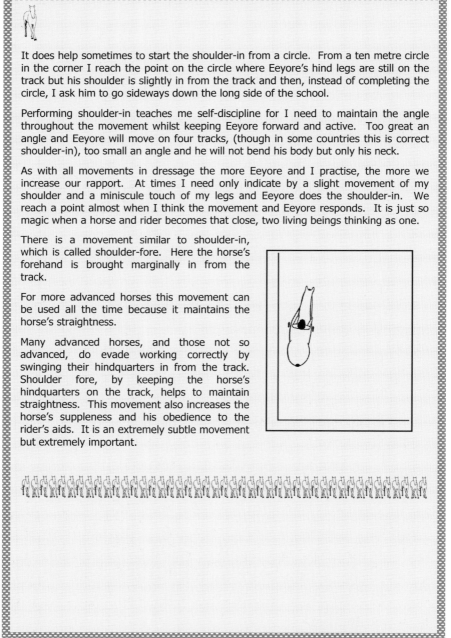

Many advanced horses, and those not so advanced, do evade working correctly by swinging their hindquarters in from the track. Shoulder fore, by keeping the horse's hindquarters on the track, helps to maintain straightness. This movement also increases the horse's suppleness and his obedience to the rider's aids. It is an extremely subtle movement but extremely important.

Before we start this circle, all twenty of us, ten pairs, need to be on the centre line together. It often happens that the forward pairs are starting the circles whilst the pairs at the back are still coming around the corner from the short side.

These circles can be a nightmare of organisation and riding. With this amount of horses, the timing has to be precise. We practise it repeatedly, with Jennie shouting at us in exasperation; it does improve with time.

 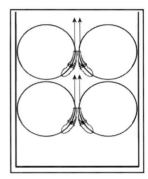

The next movement is down the centre line, split pairs at C (Jennie) and round to the long side. We wait until all pairs are on the long side then turn a 90° angle across the arena riding between each other, left to left. That means that my partner needs to be on my left and I on hers.

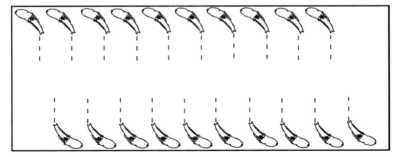

At the same time, the whole line has to cross the centre line together, so that a person standing at 'A' or 'C' sees only one horse and one rider!

 Half Pass

The half-pass is another movement that I love to do. It is similar to shoulder-in except that the horse is moving at a greater angle sideways, crossing his fore and hind legs; the horse's body is bent towards the direction of travel. Half-pass is normally performed across the school or arena.

This movement again improves the horse's suppleness and obedience, the rider's co-ordination of aids.

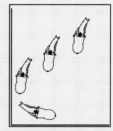

I use my inside leg around the girth area to ask for bend and forward movement, my outside leg remains slightly behind the girth to move Eeyore's hindquarters sideways. I use the inside rein to ask Eeyore to bend into the direction of travel, around my inside leg; the outside rein controls his speed. I do not want him to race across the arena, but to take long, even strides in rhythm and balance.

Bodyweight is an important aid in dressage and is used subtly. In the half-pass I use my weight by pressing my inside leg deeper into the stirrup which subtly moves my weight to the inside and allows me to move my inside hip in tiny movements towards the direction of travel.

These movements are miniscule for I must still sit centrally, quietly and softly in the saddle. A rider should never 'lean' into or away from the direction of travel in the effort to pull or push the horse into the movement.

Learning the co-ordination of the aids is important in dressage. Aids need to be used in relation to each other, but not at the same time, this would confuse the horse. For instance, in half-pass or shoulder-in, first the rider's inside leg is used for bend and forwards movement by touching the horse on his side, and then this aid is released. The outside leg is then used for sideways movement.

To enable this to happen it is important that once an aid is used it is then released. A leg aid is not applied permanently or for any length of time, it is applied then released. If a stronger aid is needed, if the horse does not obey, then a firmer aid is used, a stronger leg, then released.

If there is still no reaction from the horse, he may not understand the aid. More training is needed. If he is being disobedient then discipline is required with either a stronger, firmer aid or even a tap from the whip. The horse needs to respond from a light, instant aid, the rider should never need to apply an aid strongly or constantly.

It is much more comfortable and pleasurable for horse and rider if the horse responds to the rider's slightest aids. It is the rider's responsibility that the horse is taught to understand the aids and then is taught to obey them instantly.

With light refined aids, subtly used in co-ordination with each other the half-pass is a delightful movement. It is a joy to watch, and to ride, the horse as he moves across with long strides freely, in rhythm and in balance.

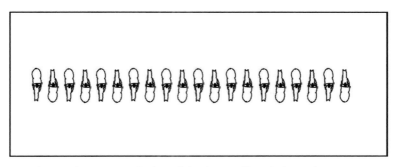

We perform the rest of the ride in walk, doing the manoeuvres singly and in pairs. Now we have to do it all again in trot.

At 10 a.m., it begins to rain but still we do not stop. The horses and riders become wet and cold but we continue. It becomes more difficult to ride the movements especially as the grass is becoming wet and the mud is churned up by the horses' feet.

Then we perform it again in sitting trot. I am not good at sitting trot, Eeyore has a bouncy stride and I find it difficult and painful to sit. This practice should improve it; I grit my teeth and sit.

Jennie yells at us about timing and we desperately try to keep together. After the cross-over we ride around the long side and up the centre line in pairs. We split at G and do a half-pass to the long side

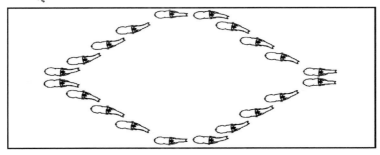

After our first half-pass to the left from G to the long side, we take one straight step, change the bend, the aids, our weight and half-pass to the right, returning to the centre line to meet our partner before we reach Jennie at 'C'.

The next manoeuvre is a ten-metre circle from the long side to the centre line, meeting our partner there and back again to the long side. Trying to keep in time with the rider opposite as well as all the riders on the same side on a ten-metre circle is a synchronistic nightmare.

The next movement is going to be fun - the scissors. For this we ride across the diagonal, from one corner of the arena to another, whilst the other ten riders, our partners, ride from the adjacent corner across the school.

We are supposed to ride between the horses coming the other way. In trot, it is a difficult enough manoeuvre; at canter it proves impossible (though the King's Troop Royal Horse Artillery do it superbly, galloping across between each other with teams of horses towing gun carriages weighing one and a half tons!). It only takes one horse to buck, one horse to back off, one to break into trot or refuse to go on and the rest are put out of time completely.

Each time we try it something happens and the result is chaos. Some horses rush across in gallop, some have to trot to avoid crashing, some go through the wrong gap, one horse bucks and refuses to go forward. Jennie wisely decides to change this movement.

Instead, we will now do a half-pass *in canter, in pairs*, with a flying change at the end on the long side of the school. Yeah right!

Half-pass in canter is difficult enough singly, I have never attempted it in pairs, nor have any of the other riders. We are certainly on a learning curve here!

The flying change is a change of leading leg. When a horse canters, one of his forelegs leads in front, normally the leading leg is the inside foreleg. For canter to the right the right foreleg will be leading. The hindleg on the same side also leads from the other hindleg. A change of leg means that the horse 'skips'; he changes his leading foreleg and hindleg at the same time.

Horses are taught to do one single change at first but as they progress, they can be taught four time changes, changing at every fourth step, three time, two time and one-time changes. These are quite natural for a horse. In the field, they will often perform flying changes when altering their direction. Eeyore loves performing changes and really becomes enthusiastic to the point where I have to stop him doing them on his own, without my aids!

In our routine for this performance, we will execute single flying changes.

First, we canter on the left rein, that is, to the left so the leading foreleg is the left foreleg. We ride around the corner of the school from the short side and half-pass to the left across the school, so that we finish going to the right. At the side of the school as we finish the half-pass we ask for a flying change, the horses change their leading legs.

The flying change is a spectacular movement. The horse needs to be cantering with energy, moving freely forward. Then the change must be straight, that is the horse should never twist or swing his hindquarters around.

Again, co-ordination of the aids is vital. In canter my inside leg is positioned in the region of the girth, my outside leg slightly behind the girth. I use the outside rein to control the speed whilst with the inside rein I ask Eeyore for slight bend to the inside.

The flying change is performed when I change these aids. I reposition my inside leg backwards behind the girth; my outside leg comes forward. In co-ordination, I change the bend with the rein. I need to sit quietly and centrally in the saddle, though my hips will move to reflect the change, one hip will move forward slightly and one backward.

It is a magnificent movement to perform, particularly on a showy horse like Eeyore, who bounds into his flying changes. I really enjoy doing this movement with him.

For our routine though, I do have my doubts about doing the canter half-pass and flying change in pairs. Surely one horse will tread on or kick another horse?

Jennie starts us off. We canter in pairs around the long side of the school, and around the corners, the outside horse canters slightly faster, the inside horse slower to keep together in pace. Around the next corner we ride and onto the long side. We ask for a slight shoulder-in for one step, then change the aids and ask for half-pass. Across the arena we go in pairs, directly to the other side, now one step straight and there, flying change, amazing, we did it. Jennie must be a magician; under her instruction, we succeed!

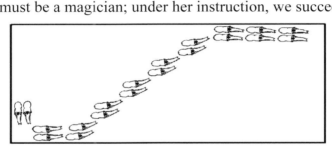

On a wet field, in a rainstorm with partners we have only just met, we achieve this difficult manoeuvre and it looks good. The flying changes are not always in time in our pairs, but at this point, we are merely glad to achieve the movement in one piece.

Around the long side and the short side in canter, then another half-pass to the right and another flying change at the side of the arena. This is going to look impressive! For some reason we perform this more complicated movement really well.

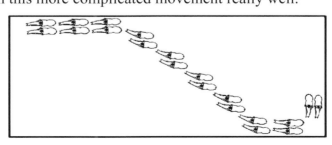

We return to trot and, in pairs, ride a three-loop serpentine, a series of loops and straight lines across the school dividing the school in three separate and equal shapes. Each pair needs to cross the centre line, in line with their partner. The inner horse needs to trot more slowly, the outer horse a little more quickly.

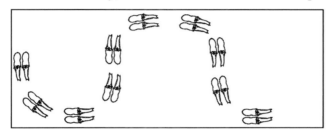

The rain is now pelting down; the horses want to turn their hindquarters into the wind. Normally when grazing in the field they protect their heads against the rain by keeping their bottoms into the wind. Now we have to ride them into the wind and rain and some of them are not pleased.

We trot and canter the whole programme again, with Jennie shouting at us through the wind and rain. The mud is muddier, the grass is becoming slimy, my poor legs and back are aching. Once more into the breach we go. Some of the movements are coming together well, but some are still out of time.

Jennie is offered a cup of tea, though I think she would prefer something stronger.

We come to a halt and have a quick breather. Then Jennie commands us to ride through it once more. The timings are still completely out, and Jennie's voice becomes louder and louder as she cajoles us into riding the circles and turns in time.

'Now! Now! Now! Come on the grey; keep up. Chestnut cut the corner. You there on the black move, move it now.'

By 11.00 a.m., it is obvious that everyone is tired, wet and cold. We look at Jennie hopefully 'please let us not do it again'.

'You can go,' she states, we all breathe a sigh of relief. 'We will practise again later.' Groan.

Two and a half hours on horseback, in a wet field with the rain sheeting down on top of us; and this is supposed to be fun!

Back to the stable with a tired, wet horse. I dismount with difficulty, as my legs are numb with weariness and cold.

Yet I cannot stop, I still need to care for my horse. It is a golden rule of horsemanship; your horse's comfort first, yours afterwards. Dripping with cold rain and stumbling about on aching legs, I rub Eeyore down with straw to help him dry. He is steaming, his body heat evaporating the rainwater. Thankfully, Sophie has already refilled his water buckets, mucked out his bed, put hay and horseage in his haynet. Eeyore gratefully drinks some water and starts to chew his hay.

I lean back against the stable wall and breathe deeply. Will I ever be able to ride a horse again? Sophie arrives at the stable from the practice field, damp and cold, but grinning from ear to ear.

'Well that was interesting,' she states. Then she sees my fatigue and grins even more. Oooh!

I shake my head, 'I am not sure I am up to this.' Strange how fit I thought I was, riding for at least one hour a day, sometimes two or three. This is wearying beyond imagination; two and a half hours riding, in the pouring rain, under the auspices of Jennie Loriston-Clarke. I would not wish this on my worst enemy. Well, maybe…..

Sophie takes over and puts the Thermatex rug on Eeyore. This rug, also known as a cooler rug, is tightly woven with small holes in the fabric; this helps Eeyore to dry and remain warm. The holes allow the dampness through; the tight weave maintains the heat of his body. If he dried without a rug in this cold temperature, he could catch a chill. The weather is now foul, rain coming down in torrents, and the ground is a sea of mud.

Lynn, in the stable to our left, looks tired and mud streaked, as does her horse Isaac. Diana on the other side, with her horse Mr. B, looks weary too. At least I am not the only one.

Once Eeyore has been rugged, fed and watered, we slowly make our way through the now muddy field to the horsebox. I change into dry clothes, as does Sophie who, having watched our performance on the field, is just as wet.

It is 12 noon and I feel as if I have done at least two days work. It is also clear that I am not well. My stomach feels as if there is an alien in there moving about of its own free will. Is it nerves, anxiety, stress or a stomach bug? Whatever, the timing is great!

The dressage group collect around Jennie Loriston-Clarke on the practice field, on a grey Monday morning.

Eeyore II, nearest to the camera, stepping out with his partner.

The Stadium with the Royal Lion and Unicorn proscenium.

Practice on foot, in the stadium in the pouring rain.
Up the centre line in pairs.

And, at the end of the routine, all halt on the centre line.

Once more round the arena in pairs, still in the pouring rain.
The Gold coach in its tent.

The Gold Coach
Front view

View from the back showing the two tritons

View from the back looking towards the front, showing the painted side panels

Temporary stables in the field

The Catering Tent

The Queen's grass verges

Isaac, Bugsy and Eeyore on their morning hack around Frogmore

One of the beautiful waterfall
scenes around Frogmore Park

The 'Heron Field', with three herons standing as still as sticks in the middle
of the ploughed earth

The Thames river: the return walk looking from Victoria Bridge towards Frogmore

Victoria Bridge over the Thames: the 'tunnel' through which we had to ride is to the left of the picture

One of the towers of
Windsor Castle

Windsor Castle in the sunset from the auditorium of the Stadium:
Wednesday evening

Never too young to learn side-saddle: junior riders exercising their side-saddle ponies.

The best day of the week, one of those high, wide, blue-sky days: Isaac, Bugsy and Eeyore in front, Sophie riding, go for a hack around the huge practice field.

Polo ponies going for their daily exercise.

Preparing for the Dress Rehearsal, the Royal Canadian Mounted Police, Mounted Police from a UK Division and the Arabs.

A 'Cowboy'

The extremely captivating and spectacular 'coloureds',
they performed the carousel in their amazing costumes

Two High Rise Gigs; these carts are extremely well balanced and easy to pull having the weight centred over the wheels.

Horseflesh in all shapes and sizes: from the elegant carriage horses, to the sturdy, handsome show hunter and the slender, dashing Arabian.

Windsor Horse Show
The Irresistible Alpacas

Show Jumping Ring

7

Monday 13th May
Day 2 the Afternoon

More practice – more rain – weary and wet

At 4 p.m., we are scheduled to catch the shuttle bus from Frogmore to Windsor Stadium. There we will practise the whole routine, ON FOOT, unmounted. The horses will stay in their stables at Frogmore.

We give Eeyore his lunchtime feed at 1 p.m., and afterwards I take him to graze in the meadow whilst Sophie skips out his bed; that is, she removes the surface droppings. Then she refills the water bucket and the haynet.

The rain has stopped for a brief period but the sky is a leaden grey and threatening.

The Gold Coach

Completely covered in 22 carat gold leaf, it shines even in the dull grey of this misty afternoon. Strange how gold never looks golden, but appears to be a gaudy yellow. The coach measures 24 feet long, (7.2 m) 12 feet high (3.6m) and 8 ft 3 inches wide (2.5 m) it weighs a massive 4 tons. The whole coach is covered with carvings and paintings.

On top of the roof are three cherubs reputed to represent England, Scotland and Ireland. They support a crown and hold the sword of state and a sceptre. Over the wheels at each corner are carvings of tritons, mythical sea gods, who have the head and torso of a man with a fish's tail. The front pair strain as they 'pull' the coach by the straps. They are blowing conches to herald the monarch of the seas. Beneath these are golden dolphins, again portraying British sea power.

The pair of tritons at the rear of the coach are carrying 'fasces' a symbol of power from ancient Rome. This symbol, in the form of a bundle of sticks, is to signify that if people stick together they are stronger and unbreakable. The idea is that one stick is easily broken whereas a bundle fastened together is almost impossible to break.

Eight palm trees, whose branches support the roof, frame the body of the coach. At the base of each tree is a lion's head decorated with the symbols of Britain's victory over France in the Seven Year's War, which was coming to its end when the carriage was built in 1762. The coach is suspended on braces designed to look like straps. They are covered in morocco leather and decorated with gilded buckles. The scallop shell at the front is the driver's footboard.

When George III ascended to the throne in 1760, he decided that he wanted a magnificent coach for his coronation and his wedding to Princess Charlotte. Sir William Chambers, one of the greatest architects of his time, created the original design for the Gold State Coach. Because it was so ornate, the coach was not finished until 1762, too late for the coronation or the wedding. It was first used for the State Opening of Parliament in November that year, an occasion for which it has been used ever since. It has also been used at the coronations of every monarch since George IV.

When it was built, the whole coach cost over seven and a half thousand pounds, a staggering sum in those days. Amazing when originally the coach gave an extremely uncomfortable ride. William IV said it made him seasick. The coach portion being slung on the two braces probably caused it to swing from side to side. The iron bound wheels did not help the suspension.

Queen Victoria flatly refused to ride in it for most of her reign stating that she hated the 'oscillations'. It probably did feel rather like a ship in high seas. After the Second World War, George VI had the coach improved by having better suspension fitted and rubber cushioning bonded onto the wheels.

The coach is pulled by eight magnificent Windsor Grey horses chosen from the eleven presently in the Royal stable. These horses are named by the Queen personally and currently include Alderney, Auckland, Britannia, Dresden, Hillsborough, Iceland, Jubilee, King's Troop, St. Patrick, Twilight and Windhoek. Twilight, a Hanoverian, is the oldest at 22 years old. These horses do not train by pulling the Gold Coach, which would be too risky; instead a specially weighted carriage is used.

We snatch a half hour in the afternoon for a nap, which helps tremendously but by now my stomach is a mass of snakes writhing against each other. How am I going to cope with an hour or so on foot? I will have to muddle through somehow; take a slug of medicine and hope it works.

It begins to rain heavily just as the shuttle bus arrives at Windsor. Even in a rainproof jacket, it is cold and miserable.

Yet, as we walk into that huge open stadium in daylight, looking at that amazing backdrop and the structures built for the lights and cameras, the realisation strikes; this massive space is reserved for the most spectacular equestrian event in living history. The bad weather seems so little to moan about.

In daylight, albeit a grey and dull daylight, the huge area is imposing. The ground is covered with a beautiful surface of sand and rubber chippings. The huge Lion and Unicorn Royal Standard proscenium is splendidly painted, with a space in its centre for the orchestra and choir.

Opposite is what appears to be a small block of flats; this is the seating for the audience of 4,000. In the centre is a portion reserved for the Royal party.

To the left of the Stadium is the Gold Coach of George III protected from the weather by a white marquee. We have the privilege of seeing it before the crowds later in the week. It was transported from London to Windsor at 4 a.m., in the morning; the first time it has left London since 1953. It was last used in 1977 for the Silver Jubilee. We are very privileged to see it here; it is usually housed in the Royal Mews. Sophie and I walk over and gaze in awe at its splendour.

We walk around the coach, stunned at its magnificence, its intricate carvings, its magnificent paintings. There in front of us is forty million pounds worth of gold and yet this means little to me. I see a rather breathtaking vehicle with the appearance of a large toy replica; it is a Cinderella's coach waiting to go to the ball.

After our sightseeing, we walk slowly to the front of the stadium. The rain is still pouring down. There are groups of people, riders and grooms sheltering in the upper seats, which are covered by a tarpaulin roof. Pools form in the metal surfacing along the front of the stands. The steps leading to the seats are covered in plastic to prevent them becoming wet and slippery. Crowds of staff are putting out flowerpots, bushes in stands and signs along the front of the seats.

Jennie Loriston-Clarke is talking with a man near the barrier between the Stadium and the stands. As we idly stroll towards her we watch the 'arena party' putting together some props for a scene.

'These are the props for the dream sequence,' states the man as we arrive at their spot. 'That is for Act 8, the one after yours.'

'It looks a complicated procedure,' I observe.

He agrees, 'Participants have no idea how difficult it is for the arena party. They have to put on and remove all the stands, pots, and any other props needed for a scene.'

We watch as the men, obviously army, struggle with some very heavy looking boxes.

The man looks around at us. 'These blocks are heavy, it usually takes quite a time to lift and transport them.'

We can see that the army guys, fit though they are, find moving the heavy blocks difficult. First they try moving one block between two men, but obviously the timing is wrong, it takes too long to remove them. So they attempt two blocks between three men. Some blocks drop, others twist around as one man is quicker than the other two.

'They have been at this for some time,' explains the man. 'They have to devise a way to lift these heavy blocks in and out of the arena. It was taking them fifteen minutes at first. These lads have to do it in less than a minute between scenes. And,' he continues. 'in the dark. There is a black out period of 60 seconds between horses going out over there,' he points to the far right of the arena, 'and horses coming in here,' he points to the left, the nearest entrance.

We watch again with renewed respect as they patiently reconstruct the blocks in the centre of the arena and attempt to remove them quickly by an alternative method. It is still not working and those poor army lads are shouted at yet again by their officer.

'And this is not all they do,' continued the man. 'These lads have to move the props for every Act, and there are 12 Acts in all including the Grand Finale. Some of the props are heavy. The props for your Dressage Group, the potted bushes marking out the arenas, have to be measured by tape for accuracy in the black out!'

He waits a few seconds while we digest this. 'Every one thinks that their Act is the most important. I tell you, without the arena party nothing would go on. They have to deal with the jumps for the pony club acts, gymkhana equipment, stands and drays for the Ascot scene just to mention a few.'

Sophie and I look at each other, the gentleman is right when he says we think only of our scene and do not often see the greater picture. We have been concentrating so hard on our own Act and its practices that we did not even consider others involved, let alone the men who have to work behind the scenes.

'Of course, it has to be the army that does this,' the man states. 'Because they are the only group of people that have the tolerance to keep doing it and the discipline not to keep questioning.'

Those words would ring in my ears throughout the next few days. Ironically, it is not long before it becomes clear that there is definitely an advantage to having a designated point of control.

After another ten minutes either the army have the solution to their problem or they give up because at last they are marking out the arenas for the dressage phase with cones.

The design for this scene is to have the Grand Prix riders in the centre with arena marked out, narrow end towards the audience, the other narrow end in front of the orchestra. The two intermediate groups are either side of the Grand Prix arena, with the long sides towards the audience.

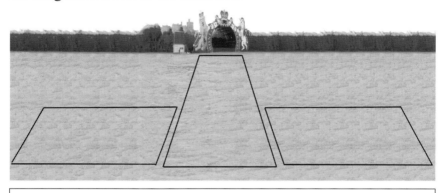

Design of arenas in the Stadium with the Grand Prix arena in centre and the two intermediate arenas either side. Please note this photograph has been graphically altered by computer.

We divide into our groups and start to 'walk' out the pattern of the movements. The Group 1 practice is in the arena to the right, the Group 2 practice is in the arena to the left.

It is fun at first, as we run through the routine, imitating the trot and canter. After the second time, with the rain sleeting down and the cold wind blowing around us, we become weary and impatient, as well as out of breath.

As time goes on and we continue to practise on foot, eventually some of the riders become irritated and argumentative; gradually the group falters and then stops. I watch as some of them huddle together in a circle, discussing the routine. One lady steps out in front and states that perhaps something else would work instead of the circles. Another argues that the circles are fine. A third suggests trying something completely different. Some other lady does not agree with that and before we know it there are several having a heated discussion on what to do or what not to do, what will work and what will not.

I cannot fathom out how they know something will succeed or fail until we try it here on the horses. Walking it out is fine to learn it, but we cannot calculate spaces correctly, or the speed of the paces without the horses.

Several people become involved with this discussion, which appears to be going nowhere. Jennie Loriston-Clarke has her own problems as she is guiding and instructing the Grand Prix riders.

Then we hear shouting and screaming from the other intermediate arena. Group 2 are almost in anarchy as a man, presuming to be in charge, states that none of the riders is taking this practice seriously enough. Indignantly, they yell, 'If we are not serious, what are we doing here now, in the rain and cold?'

Here in one arena, the members of Group 1 are gesticulating and yelling at each other. Whilst there, in the other arena, those in Group 2 are shouting at the guy whose tact is suspect.

At that moment, I look up at Windsor castle, which is watching over us like a protective guardian. The flag is flying at the top of the mast, meaning that Her Majesty is there. I imagine her watching us from one of the windows through her binoculars. I bet this is better than anything on the TV!

'Oh look, look Philip, that lot down there are having an argument. Oh do come and look.'

I can imagine her Majesty jumping up and down with delight. Better than Coronation Street or Eastenders. I giggle and receive some dark, forbidding looks. It lightens my heart though to think of it and gives me some more energy to carry on regardless!

We run through it once more, though our clothes are now becoming heavy with rain and the cold is beginning to take effect.

Halfway through we stop once more and some begin to question the movements again. Should we do a circle here? Wouldn't it be better if we….blah, blah, blah? Maybe we could do this or that? The discussion becomes more heated with arms flaying around, people shouting and arguing. Bet Her Majesty wishes she had this arena bugged. Perhaps she does!!!

This is becoming quite wild now. It never ceases to amaze me how people become irate so quickly. Two or three ladies are standing to one side; their body language is quite aggressive, hands on hips, faces pushed forwards. Others stand opposite and face them, brows furrowed. They are two warring battalions on a battlefield. Others are trying to defuse the situation. I have had enough. The rain is coming straight down like water bullets and this battle is not for me.

I motion to Sophie; we decide to leave them to it and start to make our way to the bus. As we look back the group is still discussing heatedly. It is now 6 p.m., and Eeyore needs his feed. All will be resolved once Jennie has taken control so I would prefer to return to Frogmore and look after my horse.

Thankfully another member of our group has the same idea and she, with efficient aforethought, has brought her car. She kindly offers us a lift and we drive back through the pouring rain, mud soaked, wet through, dripping and cold. My stomach has held out but only with the help of the medicine, a truly wonderful concoction. I could not have stayed much longer though and am so glad to be back 'home'.

The group returns not much later and with them comes a rumour. It is said that Her Majesty the Queen was at the acclimatisation last night. Apparently halfway through the night there was an urgent whisper that a 'Visitor' was coming. She did arrive, so they say, with a headscarf on, walking around talking to people in the stands. I do not know if this is true or not but I rather like to think so.

She is apparently looking forward to this event and becoming quite interested in how it is going to be organised. Her Majesty is not the only one!

On hearing this rumour, Sophie turns quite white. 'Oh,' she whispers in awe, 'is that who it was? I passed by a lady in a headscarf. I thought she looked familiar!'

Eeyore is fine when we arrive back at Frogmore. Despite my anxiety that he will be fretting, he looks at me over his stable door, a piece of hay in his mouth as if to say, 'Don't worry Mum I knew you would be here sometime.'

Wet and cold once again, Sophie and I return to the horsebox for a well-earned hot drink and a change of clothes. Little did we think that it could be much worse! There are times when it is better that we cannot see into the future, otherwise we would probably give up.

8

Monday 13th May
Day 2 The Evening

The Stadium – practice - catastrophe

In the timetable received prior to our arrival at Frogmore, a practice was scheduled in the Windsor arena tonight for 9.45 p.m. At dinnertime in the catering tent, we receive the news that this has now been changed. We are required to be in the arena at 10.45 p.m. With a three quarter of an hour's hack home we shall not return to Frogmore much before midnight. This is going to be a late night.

We tack Eeyore up at 9.00 p.m., and by the time we begin to hack towards Windsor at 9.30 p.m., it is bitterly cold. The rain has eased thankfully but its remnants drip from the overhanging trees and the wind has a chill factor that finds its way through the stoutest coat. The gallant grooms are again cycling behind us on wet paths covered with puddles. It is pitch black and even the lights along the route are dimmed by the damp atmosphere and make little difference to the darkness.

The hack tonight is ridden in sullen silence. We are tired, weary, aching, wet, cold and anxious. Even the horses are subdued. The Victoria Bridge still causes problems, as does the wet slippery ground beyond it. Horses still refuse to enter the 'black hole' and, when finally persuaded, they rush through, exiting onto the wet slimy ground beyond. Thankfully, there are no accidents but it gives us weary riders no respite.

Beyond the bridge, the horses, with drooping heads and tightly clamped tails, walk over the slushy mud and through the ice-cold air until within earshot of the arena and then we stop.

The ride is strung out in a long queue of horses, riders and grooms. In front of us are the Side-saddle group complete with all their attendants. Their grooms must travel with them because if any of the Side-saddle riders come off, they cannot remount without help. I have to say that riding side-saddle looks so difficult, I do admire them. How they manage to sit on with both legs on one side, particularly if the horse starts to mess about, rearing or bucking, is amazing.

In front of the Side-saddle group are some ponies, possibly children from the pony club. There are hundreds of horses and ponies here in a long line stretching from the Windsor Stadium back through Frogmore Park. Grooms and cyclists hyphenate the line, carrying extra coats, horse rugs, food and drink.

At first, the halt is a welcome break in the hack. It gives aching legs and backs a chance to relax. As time goes on though we begin to wonder just what has happened.

We wait. And we wait. And we wait. An announcement is made eventually that we will be delayed at least another half an hour. A groan arises from us all. It is now 10.45 p.m. Everyone is cold and tired, including the horses and ponies. Some of the horses in our group become restless; they begin to fidget, pawing the ground with their front legs, kicking out with their hinds.

Fortunately, where we have stopped is a space of ground between a set of toilets and a caravan. Some of us begin to walk our horses around. As time passes though, this space will not accommodate the number of horses and ponies caught up in this spot. To our left is an open space roped off, normally used as a car park on the days when the Windsor Show is open. Some of the group ask if this space can be opened now for us to keep our horses moving. There is a danger that the horses will become so cold that some of them will suffer with a chill, risking pneumonia or they could contract colic.

A steward kindly opens up the space and we all begin to walk around in a large circle. There must be sixty or seventy horses and ponies here now; dressage horses, side-saddle horses, ponies with children riders who cannot be more that six or seven years old. There are groups of coloured horses, beautifully patterned piebalds and equally eye-catching skewbalds. Walking round and round in a large circle, all these horses, ponies, riders and their attendant handlers make an amazing spectacle.

We walk in almost total silence, occasionally broken by a horse or pony who decides he has had enough and begins to trot, walk backwards or just put his head down to graze. Then there is a quiet remonstrance from the rider.

The poor grooms stand holding onto their bikes; they have to wait in that cold air in case any of the riders need help.

After another hour's wait the horses, and riders, are becoming fractious. Walking round in circles is tedious even with two or three changes of direction. Some of the horses and ponies are standing to one side; a child is crying, a mother consoling. A few of the riders have dismounted to give their horses a rest and to keep the circulation going in their own legs. I would do the same but my legs are so cold and stiff I doubt I could remount!

Those poor horses, we have been on their backs now for around two hours. The dressage horses have already done a two and a half hour stint this morning. Gallantly they are putting up with it; Eeyore seems to be coping better than I. I am becoming irritable and impatient; I can feel the emotions building up inside me.

What is causing the delay? We can hear voices over the loudspeaker coming from the lit Stadium in the distance and whilst we do appreciate the difficulties of organising a show of this magnitude, the tension increases amongst all the riders, horses, ponies and grooms waiting in the wings.

Then we hear some shouting and a steward informs us that we can continue on towards the Stadium. There is a collective sigh, as we group together and prepare to continue.

The reason for the delay apparently, so the rumour goes, is that some of the mounted police were planning to jump through a hoop of fire! The hoop however, was not large enough for the horses to jump through so they had to construct a larger hoop. To set this on fire meant contacting the Health and Safety Officer in Windsor. This, at nearly midnight, was not an easy task.

Then other groups of horses and riders, in the Stadium at the same time, did not cope well with a huge hoop of fire adjacent to them. The idea was scrapped; they wisely decided to substitute the fire hoop for a hoop of paper. This all took time; the organisers did apologise profusely.

At last we begin to move forward up the track towards the Stadium. I look at my watch, it is now just past midnight. Eeyore has had enough, he starts prancing around and being skittish. On half a ton of horse, in the middle of the night within a group of at least 60 horses, this is not what I want. Karim, next to Eeyore, has also had enough, he snorts, bends his neck and begins to trot on the spot. Both horses unsettle each other.

We line up in the Chute, that area of waiting that will become emotionally familiar to us over the next week. Eeyore is now quite bouncy, refusing to stand still or be sensible. I have a difficult time keeping him quiet, especially as we are at the back of the dressage group and he can see others in front being just as active!

A lone piper plays a mournful tune, the single notes cut across the crowds, stilling their momentum, silencing their chatter, halting the noise of speech and action. We listen carefully; pausing in life as the tune crescendos with its own heartbeat.

We are ushered into the arena through the dark shadows of the Chute. No time for anxiety now, no time to wonder if I have memorised the routine. Group 2 enter first, their faces are lit as they turn into the Stadium, the horses sharply look up and quicken their steps. This adds to our anticipation; like those having gone before, what waits for us who come after?

Our Group 1 follows the Grand Prix riders (or GP riders as they came to be known). We trot into the shining space, following the pair in front. The atmosphere drastically changes; the bright spotlights glare in our faces, the multi-coloured strobe lights move across the ground like captured rainbows. Even the music strikes our ears; no longer a distant romantic call, but a vibrant chant echoing within the Stadium.

There are crowds of grooms and family quietly applauding at the side of the Stadium to our right. In front, is a row of bright lights shining directly at us, blinding our vision and disorientating our view. For a moment our sense of distance is confused, the lights throw stark shadows in our path; the radiance changes the perspective.

We turn left and there, in front of us, is our Group 1 arena, marked off by four potted bushes, one at each corner. As Eeyore and I step into the routine, my concentration deepens to the point where there is no music, no lights, no crowds, just my horse, my partner and the horse in front. For the next seven minutes my world diminishes into a 20 x 60 metre arena, nothing else exists.

We ride our drill like automatons, stoically following the horse in front. Until finally we ride our last movement of shoulder-in, then forward into trot to the centre line and halt. I look up and salute. It is like breaking the surface of the water after a long submerged swim. I take a deep, deep breath and then smile. After all the waiting and prancing around, we as a group performed our act, with all its difficult movements, incredibly well.

The timings were out, the circles not quite circular, our movements out of synchronisation but after two and a half hours waiting around in the cold and dark, every horse behaved impeccably.

Horses are creatures of delight, patient and trusting. Considering the tiring day they have had and after just one practice on grass, those gallant creatures go into the arena and perform the whole rehearsal with equanimity, with self-confidence and composure. It is astounding.

As we walk off stage right and exit the Stadium, the whole group breathes a sigh of relief. Now we just have a 45 minute hack back to Frogmore and then rest. My legs and seat are painfully aching and my hands have gone numb.

Oh no! Not that easy. Suddenly we hear shouting.

'Come back! Turn round!'

We have to do it again.

I droop, shoulders sagging. My stomach lies heavy like iced water. I hear a groan from in front; someone else feels the same way.

No argument though, we turn the horses around and return to the Chute.

Everything is confusion here. In the dark narrow alley horses and people are milling about loosely, unsure of where to go. I look for my partner and try to find the horse in front of me. We should be at the back somewhere but all the horses and riders look so different now.

Someone shouts again. 'Get in front. Group 1 in front.'

The order has changed. Group 1 is to enter the Stadium first, followed by the GP riders and Group 2. This means we will be riding in the far arena.

As we wait in the Chute for our cue, the reasons for the alteration seep through. Group 2 in the far arena had a difficult time. It all went horribly wrong for them when the horses suddenly spied three huge dray carts, massive farm carts, at the back of their arena. This would be off-putting enough but perched on top of them were Scottish dancers!

The plan originally was to have Scottish Pipers on the drays as well as the Scottish dancers performing a reel. During practice though, it was discovered that the pipers needed both hands to play the pipes. Whenever the drays moved, which, being pulled by horses, did tend to happen now and then, the pipers tended to lose their balance and fall off!

Even without the pipers, most of our dressage horses are not used to large carts parked around an arena, with Scottish dancers whirling around on top of them. One look and for most of the horses in Group 2, that part of the stadium was a 'no go area'. Some of the horses spun around at speed; others reversed and refused to go forward. Some galloped off and headed for the other side of the Stadium.

'They have removed them,' came the cry. 'They have decided to take the drays off.'

We sigh with relief. The Scottish dancers will perform their dance on the ground.

Off we go again!

It does not work for us this time. Perhaps we are all too tired. Some of the horses begin to buck and spin round, some reverse, cannoning into others behind them. Those Scottish dancers still cause problems, with horses refusing to go near that area.

Yet amazingly for me, and this is where horses are a complete surprise, as Eeyore comes around the corner to the back of the arena, where the girls are performing, he takes one look at those Scottish dancers, breathes heavily and then totally ignores them. I am so relieved.

Perhaps our acclimatisation during the previous weeks has worked or perhaps he has become accustomed to me doing very odd things around him, dancing, jumping and shouting. He simply does not take a second look at all those girls in skirts whirling around with their hands in the air!

This rehearsal though, as a whole, proceeds horribly, with horses going everywhere but where they should. To add insult to injury, Group 2 performs beautifully in the other arena. Typical!

We exit the Stadium with our heads bowed. Another practice? No, finally we are told to return to Frogmore. There are at least five more Acts after ours so some of the participants and their horses are going to be extremely late.

We begin the hack back to Frogmore. It is now nearly 1 a.m., on Tuesday morning.

As we depart from the bright Stadium into the dim light of Windsor Park, we little know the trouble brewing in front of us.

As more than a thousand horses, ponies, riders, carriages and carts start heading back towards Frogmore, it is discovered that the gate to the tunnel under Victoria Bridge is shut and padlocked. There is no way through to the return track.   Nor are there any alternative routes because these are also blocked. All the gates to Frogmore are locked at midnight.

To make the situation worse, none of the wardens can be found. We cannot proceed, our path is blocked; we cannot ride back to Frogmore.

Fortunately it is the grooms who first discover this potential disaster. They started their return journey before us to be at Frogmore ready for our return. It is they who find the gate is locked and that the wardens have gone home. The place is deserted.

Aware that huge numbers of horses and ponies, people and riders will be coming through this area at any time, some of the grooms quickly cycle off towards Windsor to find a policeman. Thankfully, it is not true that there is never one around when needed!

After desperate explanations, the policeman gallantly manages to find a warden. Thanks to the quick wits of the grooms, the problem is solved. The gate is unlocked, just in time. If all those horses, ponies and participants, had been trapped and crammed into that small space, on a slippery hill down to the river Thames at nearly 1 a.m., in the morning, there would definitely have been trouble.

Once we pass through Victoria Bridge, the return hack to Frogmore along the riverside is more pleasant. The spotlights illuminate the pathway brightly and the tracks are broader and straighter, the riders and grooms experience a more cheerful mood.

At Frogmore, as I try to dismount I cannot feel anything below the knee, the lower leg is numb, the upper thighs and hips however feel everything. My lower back is sore and my head is just beginning to drum in time to the Scottish music. Those painful stomach cramps are the least of my problems as I slowly and painfully walk to the toilets again.

By the time we settle Eeyore down, feed, water him, then rug him up against the bitterly cold night air and tramp across the now slimy, muddy field to the horsebox, it is 2 a.m. I lie down on the bed, tuck the duvet around my sodden, aching body and begin to wonder what I am doing. Why am I not content to be an ordinary wife and mother, doing normal safe things around the house? I could be tucked up in my bed now having cleaned the house, made the tea and done the ironing.

'Goodnight,' whispers Sophie from the darkness of the luton. I mumble something; I am too tired even to cry.

9

Tuesday 14th May
Day 3

Weariness – sickness - disaster

7 a.m., arise from bed, go to feed Eeyore. Sophie and I are both too tired for breakfast today; we are hoping for a little more rest. We are disappointed. I suppose we do need the practice.

A notice is pinned to the Stable Manager's notice board.

**'All dressage riders to attend a practice
at 11 a.m., on foot in the field.'**

I could do with a hot bath, soaking for at least an hour in clean, hot water. My skin feels like leather, old leather, tanned by years of use and covered with layers of mud, dirt, sweat and grit.

It is not until I arrive at the practice, in the field by the horseboxes, on a slope, with clumpy grass, wet and slippery, that I discover that my partner has decided to move from Frogmore to Windsor.

Karim does not like being ridden under Victoria Bridge and to prevent him becoming stressed he has been moved to a stable at Windsor show ground. His stable mate, a chestnut horse in our group who is placed directly behind Eeyore in the routine, has also gone with him.

We run, literally, through the pattern again, twice. Someone then brings the music that will be playing for our Act and we run through it again.

By this time, I am feeling unwell, still suffering from the runs. I have eaten nothing and though I am drinking pints of bottled water I still feel dehydrated and tired.

The rehearsal goes well at last and with relief I start to walk towards my horsebox. We are informed that we have another practice, mounted this time, at 2 p.m.

As I feed Eeyore at lunchtime it is obvious that I cannot ride this afternoon. My visits to the toilet have increased and I am extremely sore in that area, indelicate though it is to mention it.

As I return from the toilet yet again, walking slowly to minimize the pain, I have an irreverent thought; one of those completely strange imaginings that come in times of great tiredness, on the edge of torment. I wonder if this was how the soldiers felt in Henry V's army. Why Henry V, that king of Agincourt fame? I do not know, but he is the king that came to mind. Many of his soldiers, even Henry himself, suffered from dysentery.

I can appreciate that having to constantly go to the toilet, and they had no soft paper in those days, creates extreme soreness. How could they, in agony like me, possibly have gone out to fight the

French? Imagine, running whilst feeling that fiery pain, towards an armed Frenchman who wants to kill you. I shiver with the thought of it, but oddly, it does help me to cope.

That is until I arrive back at the horsebox and feel sick. That is the last straw. The lady in the next horsebox kindly comes over to knock on our door and informs us about the practice this afternoon. I mumble something at her angrily and she anxiously asks after my health. I am not gracious in illness and mumble something else at her whilst disappearing ignobly into the horsebox. I lay down on my bed and nothing in the world could have aroused me at that point.

Even should it be decided that those who do not attend practices would be eliminated, I could not have ridden that afternoon.

There have been few times in my life when I have felt this way. Once when sailing to the Isle of Man on a Manx Steamer in a force nine gale across the Irish Sea, I was seasick. Lying on a bunk in the bowels of the ship, I could hear the bangs and bumps as the bow crashed into one wave after another. It was of no consequence to me at that moment if the ship had sunk. Sinking then would have been a mercy.

I feel just the same now. The practice goes on without me.

Later I heard that my missing partner had transported her horse over to Frogmore for the practice, only to find me missing! I apologise, but I would probably have been useless.

At that point, I felt it was quite likely that I could not ride at all for the week. I was so sore, agonisingly in pain, my stomach felt so tender.

Sleeping all afternoon was the best thing I could have done. By the evening, I felt much better. Another practice was scheduled in the Windsor Stadium that night, an 'undress' rehearsal, everything was to run exactly on time.

We have been assured that there will be no delays tonight. All the stewards have radiotelephones; if there is a delay, we will be told before we leave Frogmore. I am a bit sceptical about that, but I have to say it did work. We were not delayed at all.

Feeling much better, though still weak and sore, I decide to go through tonight and see what happens. If I do not feel sufficiently well, I will drop out.

This rehearsal will include a Finale tonight. For the Finale everyone in the act, together with their horses and ponies, return to the Stadium after the entire show. It is calculated that there could be up to a thousand horses and ponies on 'stage' at that time.

The participants, on finishing their act, are requested to remain at the back of the Stadium, behind the Lion and Unicorn backdrop, to wait for the Finale.

Tonight's practice will assess if the horses will stand quietly with hundreds of others. As Eeyore had been good during the first night's acclimatisation, I calculated that he would be fine now. I decided I would wait for the Finale after our rehearsal.

Departing Frogmore at 8.45 p.m., while the evening is still light is much more pleasant. Though it is still cloudy and cool, at least it is dry. I discover on departure that the little mare placed directly in front of Eeyore has gone lame and is not performing tonight. That is a real pity, she is a sweet little mare. To come this far and then to have to pull out would be devastating.

Since she is not here I move up to partner a bay thoroughbred type called George who is an old hand at doing these types of shows. Except for the little mare we are all riding tonight, so there will be an odd number of horses.

The ride to Windsor is becoming familiar. We depart from the horsebox field where the whole dressage group has assembled, along the pitted path by the brown wall and turn right down a tarmac lane. We continue on past the 'heron field', where during the day, herons, like black and white scarecrows, stand completely still in the ploughed earth waiting, I presume, for food. As the twilight deepens, the birds abandon their poses and begin nesting in the tall trees in the centre of the field.

We ride on until we come to some small eventing jumps, very inviting. Further on there are some fence-like obstacles on the grass verge that we think may be used for the cross-country carriage trials.

Suddenly behind us someone shouts, 'Get on the grass; get on the grass. The guns will be going off soon.'

We look around confused, we have been requested specifically not to ride on the verges or mess up the Queen's grass. Presumably, we have been given a dispensation at this point so we all ride obediently onto the grass verge. Just in time!

The Kings Troop Royal Artillery fire their guns! The noise is deafening. Even at this distance, and we must be at least a mile away from the Stadium, the earth shudders, - one: boom – two: boom – three, four, five: boom – then silence, not even a bird sings, then boom, boom, boom in rapid succession. What it must sound like in the Stadium is mind-boggling.

Some of the horses become fretful, jumping around, bucking, half rearing, imitating a bucking bronco, up at the front, up at the back. Thankfully Eeyore is completely calm, it is I who jump at the noise.

Never once in the whole week did he show, even by one twitch of an ear, that he heard the guns. I began to think he was deaf! Perhaps living in a yard surrounded by a village he is accustomed to fireworks! Typical of horses, they are all individual characters and completely unpredictable.

Under the tunnel at Victoria Bridge, glad to see there are now lights to brighten the gloom and sand to cover the stones. We walk through sedately this time.

'In the Chute', becomes the phrase of the week. We wait there listening to the previous Act and anticipating the lone piper.

George, the horse beside Eeyore is a rock. He does not move, twitch or flick an eyelid at the noise and lights. Moving up to partner him is a blessing, Eeyore seems much more relaxed in his company.

Claire, who rides him, has a beautiful position and I try to emulate her. She looks so good on her horse; perhaps she has the right shape, long slim legs, and a slim body. Me with my shorter legs will never look as good as that, still no harm in trying.

She also gives me advice on how to ride at these events. 'Sit deeper and heavier in the saddle,' she suggests. 'Keep your horse's head right up the tail of the horse in front then he cannot look around or spook.'

I am nervous and no matter how I try to hide it, Eeyore senses it, he knows me so well. My seat muscles tense and my thighs are stuck to the saddle like clamps.

I breathe deeply, blowing air out through my mouth in quick gasps. Then I try to keep my mouth open slightly to prevent my jaw from stiffening like a rock.

'Keep the horse well up into the bridle,' whispers Claire. 'If he does shy or spook put your leg on and hold him with your reins.'

The lone piper starts his tune, someone shouts from behind, 'Go in, go in now.' Others are shouting from the front. 'They are not ready yet.' A scream from behind, 'Never mind anyone else get in there.'

Eeyore becomes tight under the saddle; he can feel the tension. Just as he begins to feel jumpy, I push his nose into the tail of the chestnut in front and it works. Keeping him firmly between my legs and hands, right up the bum of the one in front, we enter the Stadium. He does not shy at the poster barriers as he did the other night.

So far so good, trot down the arena, towards the audience, lone piper still blowing his pipes. Now turn to the left across the front of the Stadium into the spotlights. People begin to applaud; the sound is louder than previous evenings, more like a clap of distant thunder.

Sophie, who has taken the shuttle bus tonight because she is suffering from saddle soreness from her bike, is somewhere out there in the blackness of the auditorium.

We cross the Stadium and arrive at our arena. The music is still not playing the tune for us to start so the front pair decide to continue riding around the arena in pairs rather than splitting at the end of the centre line. We trot the length of the school and back up the centre line.

Pause and silence, the lone piper has stopped but the Act music has not started. We continue riding down the centre line in silence. This time we must begin our routine. We divide at the end of the centre line; Eeyore and I go to the right, towards the audience. I feel Eeyore pull back as he senses the people out there in the black, so I put my right leg firmly onto his side and make him trot around the corner into the shoulder-in down the long side.

Up the centre line once more and into an individual ten metre circle, to the long sides of the school. The synchronisation is completely out as we arrive at the centre line at different times. Up the centre line, turn right again, now cross over going left to left, that was adequate, the timing could be better, we all need to arrive on the centre line together.

I begin to relax a little; Eeyore is going well. Down the centre line again and turn left towards the massive screens at the back, which are showing our ride, and the Scottish dancers doing their own thing.

Suddenly all hell breaks lose. The chestnut in front of Eeyore stops dead. Whether he sees the dancers, or himself on the huge screen at the back of the Stadium, is not clear, but just at that moment the bagpipe drummers do their ratatatat ratatatat, extremely loudly, sounding just like shots from a rifle.

The chestnut has had it; he speeds backwards straight into Eeyore's face, spins round and gallops across the arena, cutting through the ride. Eeyore stops and spins round as well. I can feel my heart pounding as I sit on half a ton of horseflesh about to burst into speed.

Quick take control. I hold the reins more firmly and twist Eeyore round. Pressing my heels into his sides, I encourage him to follow the appaloosa in front. We just reach the appaloosa's bottom when he does the same thing. He sees the screens or the dancers in the spotlights, stops, half rears, bucks and steps backwards straight into Eeyore's face.

Now Eeyore has had enough. The rider of the appaloosa quickly gains control and pushes her horse onwards. But the damage is done. Eeyore spins around again; I stop him and turn him round. He backs up away from the track and lifts his forelegs off the ground slightly in a half rear. I feel myself losing control quickly. Eeyore feels me tighten in fear and he starts to go backwards very fast.

No, I scream inside, this is exactly what I have feared. I am on the verge of panic when suddenly, and it could not have happened at a worse time, one of the horses at the back of the ride decides to bolt, it gallops top speed straight past Eeyore and me. Eeyore stops to look; I hold my breath in anticipation of him bolting too. I can feel the muscles in his hindquarters bunch in preparation for a jump forwards.

It is at those points in time, when all hell breaks loose, that you dig something up from inside. 'Get a grip,' I told myself. I have been frozen in time, in a blind panic, my mind has gone into oblivion, stunned into complete stillness and then it happens. From somewhere I receive an energy surge, 'I must do this, I must do this, I cannot let go now. For Queen and Country and all that. ' I use the instant of Eeyore's hesitation and start kicking for all I am worth.

I release my legs and again go kick, kick, kick on Eeyore's sides. It is the same feeling as when you are swimming and it turns into drowning. You go down, once, twice, and the third time you know you have to do something or you are finished. It is then that you lash out with arms and legs to swim. I know that if I do not get hold of the situation now, I will either fall off, be bolted with or be turned out of the ride.

I am holding tight onto the rein to stop all Eeyore's energy bursting out in front, so I cannot stroke him. I use my voice instead. As confidently as I can I speak to him, 'Come on Eeyore. We can do this together.'

He listens to me, thank goodness, oh you little beauty. We begin to follow the appaloosa, leaving a space for the chestnut who eventually comes across from somewhere to quietly fill the gap. I breathe again.

It is only a few seconds later that I realise that we are not where we should be. Where are we? This is not correct. We are not supposed to be here now. Jennie's insistent instructions fill my mind, 'follow the horse in front; even if things go wrong, keep in the ride.' That is what we will do, follow the horse in front and hope for the best.

We later learn that the two riders in the front of the ride, the leaders, had taken the wrong route. What is strange in a ride of this size is that the awareness does not stretch beyond your immediate surroundings. The concentration is all on the bum of the horse in front and your partner; nothing else matters. For those first few nights of rehearsals, I was concentrating so hard and focusing on the ride that I did not even hear the music.

We continue despite being in the wrong place and soon we are working towards our penultimate movement, the shoulder-in together on the long side of the school facing the audience. Then, in time with each other, we ask the horses to trot forwards towards the audience and halt somewhere in the region of the centre line.

Just as we reach the line, a chestnut horse to my right decides to rear. Straight up the mare goes on her hind legs, the exact minute she reaches the line. The rider on top does well to stay on; he has no warning. This does have a rippling effect through the line of horses; there is a bumping motion that passes along the line. We try to salute on horses that are spinning, stepping sideways, reversing speedily, snorting and pawing the ground. It is difficult to release one rein for a salute when the horse underneath is cavorting to his own tune.

So the 'undress' rehearsal, for our Group, was a disaster. We even finished after the Grand Prix (GP) riders, a thing unknown and unacceptable. The GP riders do a passage, (pronounced passARGE) that is, a slow expressive trot, down the arena towards the audience and a piaffe, (trot on the spot) until the intermediate rides have finished. Then Jennie Loriston-Clarke takes a step forward on her stallion, Humbug, and salutes. That's the cue for us all to salute. Because our ride took an incorrect route tonight we were well out of time and finished after Jennie had saluted. Whoops!

We quickly ride forward, turn, join our partners and trot off to the left out of the Stadium. The sigh of relief is audible from all the riders. What a night! At least nobody fell off. We did hear that one of the Side-saddle group parted company with her mount when the horse decided it was time to call it a day, or night, and exploded in front of the screens.

'All those going home, go to the right,' a loud voice announces as we exit the Stadium. 'Everyone staying for the Finale go to the left.'

Eeyore and I go to the left and stand next to George behind the Stadium. At first, all seems fine. Eeyore is calm, standing still, his head and ears drooping, which means he is relaxed.

We stay there for about ten minutes and then jazz music starts to play loudly in the tent next to us. Eeyore pricks up his ears at this and starts to tense up through his body. It does not help when children with skirts and wiggly things on their heads start jigging about to the music. He becomes quite agitated, backing up and side stepping in a circle.

Under normal circumstances, loud music does not worry him; he loves working to music. The yard at home always has the radio on, blaring away through the stables. Yet, for some reason, he really becomes heated up when the jazz starts.

It becomes more difficult to keep him still. His neck becomes stiff and tense, he starts to paw the ground.

Then suddenly he springs to one side. I look and there in the shadows is the household cavalry, the light glinting from their metal helmets. Row upon row of them wait silently, their shadowed figures like ghosts from some ancient war.

Eeyore really starts to move now, walking round and round in circles, jigging on the spot. No matter how I try to calm him, stroking his neck; talking to him, he becomes more stressed by the second.

All eyes are upon us; everyone is looking at us, as though they are waiting for us to disgrace ourselves. My imagination plays tricks on me and, as I look at their faces, they look evil; it appears as if they are telepathically causing our distress. As in one of those horror movies when the evil ones say nothing but look at the victim, willing him to die. I shake my head, it is enough that Eeyore is rapidly losing his cool, I must hold onto my sanity or we are lost.

Eeyore's head rises higher, his neck is as solid as rock. I can feel the muscles go rigid under his saddle, like steel bars.

What really finishes him off though is the Lancers. As soon as he sees those men sitting on their horses holding large poles, that is it. We speed across the space, narrowly missing some people and horses. I have little control over him; he is doing his own thing.

One rider on her horse turns to me and says 'I am not sure you should take him into the Finale, if he is like this out here it will be ten times worse in the Stadium.' She is right. The dressage riders for the Finale are to stand next to the Military Band. Perhaps this is not such a good idea.

It is a pity, though. It may be the enclosed space, the soldiers quietly waiting in the shadows, the kids dancing around, the jazz music or a combination of everything. Maybe he does not want to repeat that long wait last night. I feel as if I am sitting on a time bomb and I decide not to risk going in for the Finale. All I want to do now is to escape from here and calm him down.

But where should I go? I have no idea of the way home, always having walked with a crowd. I have never been behind the scenes before and the exits are all blocked with cavalry, troopers and other riders waiting to enter the Stadium.

Those riders who have already gone home have taken a different route tonight. Instead of turning to the left and walking home beside the road, they have gone to the right and around the show ground, I do not know that way. Fear hits my stomach like a sharp icicle. Whichever way I go I will be on my own. It could be even worse when Eeyore is taken away from the 'herd'.

10

Tuesday 14th May
Day 3 The Evening

Lonely terror – pain and sorrow

What should I do now? First thing is to dismount and lead him, which shows how wound up he is because I rarely feel safer on the ground than aboard.

I search around for a steward to ask for help and to show me the way back to Frogmore, but I cannot find anyone. Eeyore is becoming more agitated and I fear that he may become too much to handle. There are children, adults, ponies and horses everywhere. Holding onto a large black horse about to blow his top is not my idea of fun or safety.

I lead him away from the crowd, out to the left where we have exited previously, just hoping for the best.

In the dark, narrow lane of the Chute, it is even more frightening. The shadows are packed full of waiting cavalrymen. There are Lancers and Dragoons; the Kings Troop with their guns attached to teams of horses. There are dark skinned soldiers with brightly coloured uniforms. Rank upon rank of cavalrymen, row upon row of uniformed gunners, Household Cavalry, mounted policemen, all waiting in anticipation. Only the soft sounds of horses breathing with the occasional chink of a metal bit, breaks the dark, heavy silence.

The atmosphere is brimming with excited, anxious anticipation. This feels like the moment just before a battle, 'with shining eyes and bated breath, we all await the dance of death'. The waiting lines are silent, poised, ready for action. Eeyore and I can taste the tension.

Eerily, not a sound emanates from those masses of waiting men. They stand like statues, not a muscle moves. Eeyore and I walk amongst them, like living beings through the world of the dead. We feel we are being watched yet no eye follows us along the path.

It is fearful, leading a prancing black horse towering above me through crowds of silent horsemen. I talk quietly to him and stroke him, assuring him that I am there with him. He snorts and bends his neck, looking down at me, his brown eye surrounded by white fear. He seems to grow taller by the second, rising to 17 and 18 hands high.

I move him over to the grass verge to place myself between him and the soldiers, positioning myself between him and the threat.

I pray that the Finale does not start yet, that this great horde, unstoppable as the ocean wave, does not launch forward directly into us, or we will be lost. If this crowd begins to move, I could not hold Eeyore; he will go.

We walk on through the massed ranks, row upon row of soldiers, guns on carriages, horses nodding their heads and pawing the ground, occasionally rattling their bridle with impatience.

Then suddenly, as if reaching the abrupt end of a forest, Eeyore and I emerge from the last rank out into an empty space.

The world is silent again as we stand at the edge of a floodlit green field, beyond which is the night, dark and uninviting. There is no-one around, no-one to turn to, no-one to ask for help.   I let Eeyore eat some grass hoping this will calm him down. What to do now? I am lost and alone, with a large horse who could panic at any moment.

Two people begin to walk towards us. It is my original partner, the one who rides the black horse Karim and her friend who rides the chestnut.

'Are you alright?' she asks. Obviously I am not, lost, alone and holding a very frightened horse. Kindly she indicates the way home, across the green field to the purple horsebox, then turn right along the path.

I look into the distance; the green field is lit by one huge spotlight. It looks alien, spectral, uninviting. Around its periphery, the night is black and silent, as threatening as a waiting predator.

I decide to ride Eeyore again; I do not relish a walk home holding onto him on my own through the miles to Frogmore. As soon as I mount, I can feel his back go into spasm; any second now he is likely to explode. With his stress and tension, possibly soreness in the back through all the hours of riding, he feels unsafe.   I dismount again and proceed to lead him.

We cross to the purple horsebox and, thankfully, I recognise the path. At least I now know the way home. I lead Eeyore on, through the mud, down the slight slope and under the Victoria Bridge. A steward is there and he bids me goodnight. He has to be joking! He is the last person I will see.

It is nearly eleven o'clock at night; the path is completely empty, there is not a soul around. Here I am in a lonely spot, in an unknown environment by the River Thames. Just me and my horse.   The floodlit path throws shadows all around, the trees seem to bow towards us, the night sounds are so clear.   The whisper of the night breeze, the plip plop of water being moved by an unidentified source, the slippery sliding sounds of leaves and grasses as though someone is following.

Against this whispery background, the sounds of my boots and Eeyore's metal shod hooves clip clopping on a tarmac path are like gunshot cracks in the night.

We walk together along the towpath with the river passing by, nonchalantly, uncaring, reflecting white and orange lights from the opposite bank.   The shadowed troughs of the small waves, the bulrushes by the bank, all potential hiding places for those in wait.

I feel so alone, listening out for any other footsteps particularly if they are running up behind us.   I imagine knives in my back, hands around my throat.   I hope that a large black horse is enough to deter anyone with evil intent.

Then we turn away from the river and pass between fields of grazing cattle, through woods where the trees overhang, the shadows dart from under the bushes.   Once or twice Eeyore shies at something he imagines is lurking there to pounce, so I change sides to be between him and the danger.   I am the head of the herd; I am the one who has to protect him.

We are halfway home when Eeyore stumbles and treads on my right foot putting his whole weight on my boot.   It is agony and within a few steps, I know I have broken my little toe.   It is a pain I recognise, the feeling of bone scraping on bone.   I have been trodden on by horses before, I know the signs.   We have miles to walk yet.   Nothing to do about it except lighten my steps on that side; keep my weight as much as possible off that foot.

I have no mobile phone because I thought it was unsafe carrying it in my jacket whilst riding in the show.   Eeyore looks at me with his big brown eyes, he looks so anxious; I must put on a brave face for him.

'Don't worry, we'll be alright.' I hope I sound more confident than I feel. I am not even sure I am on the right road; we could end up anywhere.

A sign looms up out of the darkness, '**Frogmore Return**'. Thank goodness. I stroke his neck and keep my hand on him guiding him and reassuring him.

At least the night is dry even if the breeze is cold. It is odd that we meet no-one at all, surely the ride should catch up with me after the Finale? I keep looking behind but an empty lane stretches out into the dark.

We clip clop over a bridge and stream, and pass a little brick house. There are lights shining from inside penetrating the darkness but not my loneliness. It makes me feel more alone. They in their world of laughter and voices, light and warmth, us in our world of silence and cold, dark shadows and fears.

The darkness and pain depresses me; I feel tears stinging my eyes. I experience one of those moments when life begins to slide irretrievably down that long black hole. Eeyore snorts, 'do not give up now Mum, I need you'. I sniff strongly, breathe deeply, keep my ears and eyes open, survival.

Another sign sends us off to the right; I would have chosen the path directly in front. It is darker here, the bushes encroach to the side of the lane, rhododendrons, laurels, thick green foliage, sounds of scuttling insects or animals, places of hiding and ambush. Walk on, walk on, will this lane never end?

I am almost halfway home when I make the decision. Eeyore has been through so much these last two days; I am asking too much of him. Not only do I risk injuring him physically, the riding must have made his back sore, but I risk breaking the trust we have between us.

It has taken me three years to build up that trust between my horse and I and, nothing, nothing, not even riding in front of the Queen is worth destroying that trust.

When I bought him he was quite a nervous character. He was terrified of whips; he would not allow anyone to touch his poll, the part between his ears. If he did something incorrect in the school, his body would immediately tighten like a coiled spring, preparing for a reprimand.

He had come from a competitive home; being competed at a high level needs strict training. This is not wrong in itself, horses do need discipline; too little discipline is as harmful, if not more so, to both horse and rider. In highly competitive environments though, horses are sometimes too firmly controlled.

I had spent the last three years encouraging him to relax, letting him know that if he made a mistake he would not be hit. Now I could stroke him all over with a whip. I even encouraged him at times by tapping him with the whip on the hindquarters and I had so gained his trust that he was quite relaxed about it. I could stroke his poll; even gently 'pull' his ears.

We had grown so close through patience and time, we had created so much trust between us; was it worth it to risk all that?

Beside it is making me ill. Whenever I wait to enter the Stadium, I feel sick with the anticipation, the adrenalin pumping through my body. I have not been able to eat much since Sunday and have already lost four pounds in weight. I am not anxious about the loss of weight but that constant sick feeling is tiring me out.

So the dark shades of doubt pervade my mind, even as the shadows creep along the path in front of us.

If I did give up what would I tell everyone? All those people coming to see me ride, Derek, my husband, Sophie, Martyn and Helena, my children, four of my friends. What do I tell all those back at the yard who are obviously proud of me? My mother, who could not be here but who is waiting expectantly to see me on T.V. What would I say?

Eeyore snorts and curves his neck around, looking at something in the bushes. I hear a scratching sound, small enough not to threaten us. 'Come on old boy, I am here.' I stroke his neck and he bows his head down rubbing the side of his face gently on my jacket.

My toe is throbbing with red pain, swollen and pressed against the side of my boot. I limp and pray Eeyore will not tread on me again.

My thoughts return to the burning question, what could I say to everyone if I pull out? To take the pressure off I begin to think of excuses; a broken toe, sickness, the horse could not cope. The truth is I am scared; I am frightened that either I will fail or my horse will bolt with me and I will fall off in front of the Royal Family. I do not want to lose face.

We enter the woods, lit by powerful lights, silvering the underbelly of leaves, bringing into sharp relief the protruding skeletal arms of branches.

Think though, apart from tonight Eeyore has behaved well. True, we have had the disaster tonight, but apart from that he has not bolted with me, galloped off, reared or bucked. He is just tense and tight tonight.

We traverse the crossroads and walk straight ahead. I look at my watch; it is almost midnight. Am I still on the right track? Where are the horses from the Finale? They must catch up with me soon. This is odd.

Yet how can I continue to put Eeyore through it after this evening? It is not fair on him to push him through this, I have to give up; there is no other alternative.

Into the straight lane bordered by flat grass and a yew hedge, down to the tent where there may be a soldier on sentry. The tent flaps gently and Eeyore eyes it with distrust but I change sides again, painfully, to put myself in the firing line. He relaxes.

The last corner, the stone pitted lane edged by the brown wall. It is the darkest here, no lights at all. Only the pale fringe of roses on the wall tells us we are moving forward.

Then halfway down, the eye-stinging brightness of a powerful floodlight by the stables blinds us. The darkness here is even more intense as it shrinks back into itself before the light.

Eeyore hides behind me, I encourage him with words, the sound of my voice. Through the blackness we walk slowly, the light and safety just ahead.

Even if we do decide to drop out we have certainly achieved walking home together in the dark, along a lonely road in unknown territory and we have arrived relatively safely, apart from a small broken bone.

I have never been so pleased to see a row of temporary stabling. My foot is now agonising and my legs ache from the walk and the cold.

We turn the corner and walk towards Eeyore's stable. Then I cry out. There she is, there is Sophie. She dashes up to us and hugs me tightly; then she hugs Eeyore flinging her arms around his neck.

'Thank God, thank God,' is all she can say. She must have been worried about us. Were we that long?

'You have no idea how worried I have been,' she states as we lead Eeyore to his stable. Me too!

'All I heard,' she explains, 'is that one of the horses in the Dressage Act suffered colic and had to be walked home. 'Course, nobody knew which horse or from which group.'

She looks at both of us with concern. 'Is Eeyore alright?'

'Yes he's fine. He became agitated before the Finale so I walked him home.' I explain wearily.

Her relief is obvious. She escorts us to Eeyore's stable and relates her side of the story.

After looking for us in the Finale, she had walked backstage and desperately searched for us, but of course, we were not there. In panic, she procured a lift from the gentleman who runs the Shuttle buses; he had told her about the horse taken ill. Once she arrived back at the stables she had an anxious wait.

'I was so, so worried. My dear, dear Eeyore,' she is almost in tears. Eeyore whickers at her and rubs himself on her arm.

At least he had not suffered colic; that would have been terrible.

The horse with colic came from the Side-saddle group. They had walked back to Frogmore on their own. If only I had known, yet I had not seen or heard them.

Sophie leads Eeyore into his stable and untacks him; he relaxes visibly. She places his rug on him to keep him warm and gives him some feed, he dives into that, not much wrong then! She has already mucked out his stable and found another bale of shavings from somewhere; filled his haynet, cleaned and refilled the water buckets.

Within a short time, Eeyore is tucked up warmly in his stable munching on his hay. He now looks peaceful, calm and relaxed. I lean against the stable door and sigh deeply; it has been a tiring and painful night.

Then a wave of weariness overwhelms me and I slide down to sit on the grass. With bowed head and tears filling my eyes, I feel the full agony of that broken toe, feel the coldness of shock; I begin to shiver uncontrollably.

Sophie helps me up but by now I can hardly walk. Leaning on her heavily, I limp to the horsebox where I remove my boot carefully. The toe is bent in a strange manner, bright red and very swollen; it is painful and throbbing violently. What an end to a horrible night!

Sophie places her arm around my shoulders and at that, my lowest point, I cry.

We cannot continue, the last two days have been too much for me; I am not up to it. I do not have either the strength or the ability.

Sophie holds me as I release all the pent up pain, fear, anxiety and weariness.

Then in her quiet, calm voice she tells me 'I was speaking to the director of the shuttle buses tonight,' she says. 'He gave me a lift back because the shuttle bus had not arrived. You know what he said?' I shake my head.

'He said that he has been to many of these events over the years. And at every occasion there is one night, either the dress rehearsal or the night before that they call 'buggery night' and they call it that because everything that can go wrong will go wrong.

This night is the night when everyone loses their confidence; everyone goes home swearing they will not do it.' She pauses; perhaps it is not just me after all, perhaps I am not alone.

Sophie continues, 'He said that what is amazing is that always, always, by some miracle it all comes together.'

I look at her in disbelief.

'It's true,' she adamantly tells me. 'You were not the only one tonight to have problems. Do you know that one of the racehorses bolted? It went ballistic, speeding round the arena. The jockey fell off and landed right on top of three men, stewards I think. Thankfully, nobody was badly hurt but the jockey did go to hospital.'

'And some of the Side-saddle horses bolted too. One of their riders fell off.' Then she grins wickedly, 'and as for one of the mounted police…what an embarrassment! One of them fell off but what was worse, he simply could not remount. Honestly,' she nods violently, her eyes bright. 'Try as he might he could not get back on the horse. The horse kept moving around, backing up, then it ran off and he had to chase it,' she tries hard to suppress the giggle.

'Imagine if that had happened to you!' she adds. 'Ooh yes, and the GP riders got their movements wrong. And that was only what I saw. It was murder out there tonight not just for you.' I feel better but am still not truly convinced.

'Look,' Sophie wraps her arms around me once more. 'Get a good night's sleep and see how you feel in the morning. We are both tired out right now and in no shape to make decisions.' We drink some hot chocolate, which helps and then we prepare for bed.

'What about your toe?' She looks at the bright red thing on the end of my foot. 'Not much we can do,' I reply knowledgably. 'Last time the hospital did not even strap it up. I shall see how it is in the morning; perhaps I can bandage it to the other toes. We'll see.'

Nothing could keep me awake, not a broken toe, or depression. As soon as my head touches the pillow I am out. Thank goodness tomorrow is another day as the cliché goes. We'll see what happens tomorrow.

III

Autopsies – more practise – more changes – success!

It is at that moment of waking with the light streaming into the room that the feeling hits, something is wrong. The light is coming from the wrong direction; the window is in the wrong place. An instant of panic before recognition; the horsebox, of course, I remember now.

When I move my foot I remember other things too, that walk back last night. My legs are aching, the muscles bulging with stiffness. I groan and this wakes Sophie.

It is 8 a.m., we are late, late for Eeyore's breakfast. I quickly sit up on the bed and groan again. My whole body is pained. What happened? Did Mike Tyson win?

The toe is a strange shade of puce, a deeper shade of red; it does not look good. I try to stand but only manage half way.

'You lie down, Mum,' Sophie turns and wriggles out of the luton. 'I'll do Eeyore today. You are in no shape to do anything.'

I put the kettle on the little hob and brew some coffee.

On Sophie's return she informs me that Eeyore is well, he could not wait for his breakfast! Always a good sign if a horse will eat; the moment to panic is when they refuse food, that is when something is radically wrong.

Horses are 'trickle' eaters, that is, they are constantly eating; their gut needs to be filling with food all the time, they can eat 22 hours out of 24! Unlike cows they cannot regurgitate and chew the cud, the food goes right through their digestive tracts and, as grass is a difficult food to digest, so they have to keep eating it to extract the nutrients.

Last Christmas Eeyore cut his left foreleg and had to be confined to his stable for a week or so. Unfortunately at the same time I had the 'flu and was confined to bed. With his injury and pining for me, Eeyore slid quickly into depression and refused to eat. They desperately tried to tempt him with carrots and apples, but it was not until I was able to visit him at the stable and walk him out in hand for some grass, that he began to recover.

Another time I had moved him to a new stable just as I went on a holiday: bad timing. With the unfamiliar surroundings and missing me for a week, he refused to eat. Once I returned, he began to tuck in again. So I know that as long as he is eating, he is OK.

Sophie tells me that there is a meeting of all the dressage riders at Jennie's horsebox at 9 a.m. I groan. Perhaps I will be asked to leave. I can feel myself becoming morbid again.

'Do you really want to give up?' Sophie can see the despair in my face. 'Why don't you do the Dress Rehearsal tonight, see how it goes. If Eeyore does get upset then call it a day, yeah?' She sounds so practical.

'I'll go to this meeting and see what they say.' I acquiesce. 'It may all be decided for me. If I am not asked to leave I will do it tonight and see how it goes. If Eeyore is still uptight and stressed then I will pull out.' I feel much better now that the decision is made.

'Have another coffee,' advises Sophie. I smile, what would I have done without her?

I walk down the hill towards Jennie Loriston-Clarke's horsebox. Despite the aches and pains, I feel better. The stomach cramps have gone and I do not feel dehydrated. A weak sunlight brightens the morning and the breeze feels warmer, more encouraging.

Jennie's box is difficult to miss as it is painted with a Union Jack. By 9 a.m., everyone is there, waiting. Jennie walks up to us and looks at us all. We feel like shamed school kids.

'Well that wasn't too good was it?' Her voice sounds stern yet she has a smile on her face. 'You're all supposed to be good riders, what went wrong?' No-one answers. She looks around at us one by one. 'We've been watching the video of it.'

Oh no, here it comes. Jennie turns to the two riders in leading file. One of them apparently had taken the totally wrong route and this is why we ended up in the wrong place. Some of the riders had followed her, being told to carry on following if anyone went wrong. Others unaware of the mistake had continued on the right route. The horses had then become mixed up and that particular leading horse finished up halfway down the ride.

To add insult to injury the other leading horse had stopped and reared halfway through the performance, which meant the rest of us had come into walk instead of maintaining the trot.

The horse in front of me had spooked (I knew that), spun and bolted off through the ride, creating havoc with the back riders. Then one of the back horses had bolted right through the front of the ride. This was the horse who had passed me.

One of the second pair had reared as it entered the Stadium and been reluctant to go forward. The chestnut who had reared the minute it reached the centre line affected the horses around it and they had spooked and backed off. That was Group 1. Group 2 had totally missed out a whole section of their ride, finishing especially early in front of everyone else.

The night to end all nights, it appears. Despite all the drama and upset, I feel better. Others had suffered too last night. At least Eeyore, despite being bumped into by two horses, had carried on and completed his ride. I began to feel quite proud of him. I had no idea that such dramas and tragedies were taking place around us.

'We will have to make some changes then,' states Jennie.

The leader who had taken the incorrect route is placed further back in the ride. The chestnut, fifth in line will take over; the young girl rider is a confident rider. The other leader is asked to move, but she assures Jennie that her horse can cope and the incident will not recur.

The second pair are moved to third and the two greys in third place are moved up to second. Not only are the leading horses in a dressage team of paramount importance, they must be bombproof, forward going and obedient, it is vital that the second pair is sound and obedient too. If anything occurs to the first pair, the second pair will have to take over and continue.

It is also essential that the back pair of riders are competent. They are constantly playing 'catch up'. For some reason, even when the front of the ride is going slowly, the back pair are always going at speed to keep their correct distance. It is this pair that have to ride for their lives just to keep in pace.

Jennie looks at us sternly once more, yet around her eyes is the hint of laughter, and her mouth lifts up at the corners. I have a feeling that stern and disciplined as she is, and has to be, just below the surface is compassion, understanding and a huge sense of humour!

'Tonight is the dress rehearsal,' she remarks starkly. 'We must get it right tonight.'

Jennie then states that there will be another practice on grass at 2 p.m., this afternoon. We do need all the practices possible.

I am feeling so much better that I decide to go on a hack with a couple of the riders, one from our group and one from Group 2. Bev lives near to me, she is a lovely person and her horse Wonderberg (Bugsy is his stable name) knows Eeyore well.

The other lady, Lynn, also lives not far from me. Her horse Isaac is in the next box to Eeyore. It was while Sophie and I were grooming Eeyore yesterday that she came around and looked over the stable door.

'What did you say his name is?' she asked looking at Eeyore.

'Eeyore II,' I replied. I knew what was coming.

'Oh yes,' she exclaims, 'That's Eeyore II, I thought I recognised him. I looked at him when he arrived and he looked familiar.' She looks at him with shining eyes. 'Then when I heard you calling him Eeyore, that was it. I have seen him at competitions. He's beautiful, how did you get him?'

Here we go again. It does have its disadvantages riding a famous horse, everyone expects so much more skill from the rider. The case is that Eeyore is my schoolmaster, he is teaching me. I am proud of him though and it does increase my sense of pride at having such a talented horse.

Sophie accompanies us on her bike as does Bev's sister Vanessa. We walk around the tracks through Frogmore Park, keeping to the route we take at night to Windsor. It is lovely to be on Eeyore without any pressure. He is relaxed and enjoying it at last. Despite a throbbing toe in a tight boot, we both so enjoy that ride. The sun comes out, we can see the herons in the 'heron field', and watch the boats on the river. There is so much more to see in daylight. For an hour, we hack at a slow walk and then return Eeyore to his stable for his lunch.

An incident happens then that makes me think about my situation. Bemoaning my fate with a broken toe, aching back and legs, as I return from the catering tent a lady walking behind me trips over and falls flat on her face. It is quite a shock; she goes down like a felled tree. Walking over, I ask if she needs help, she is clutching her side; her face is twisted in pain.

'No I am fine,' she insists though she looks extremely pale. 'I have had a terrible week,' she states. 'Last week I fell off my horse and broke a rib, my side hurts like hell.' I look at her in amazement.

'But are you supposed to ride?' I ask.

'No, not really, but I was not going to miss this week.'

'Do you want to sit down and rest?' I am quite anxious about her.

'No, I'll be fine.' She gives me a weak smile and hobbles off holding her side with both arms. What courage and determination.

When I am down and out, convinced I am at the bottom, there is always someone worse off. Makes my broken toe sound silly! I shall not moan about it again!

Even before the 2 p.m., practice time, the rumours are flying around, about people being asked to stand down, others resigning; about changes of partners, even rumours of changes within the two rides.

One gentleman approaches my horsebox and angrily shouts at us about having more practices, more changes.

'How do they expect us to change rides now?' he exclaims waving his arms around. I shrug my shoulders; he does not really want a reply. He has heard that riders are going to be swapped between the two rides. He is so incensed that he is talking to me as though

I am his best friend, even though I have never met him before as he is in Group 2.

Eventually when he calms down I advise him to wait and see what happens; wait until we hear something definite, Jennie will do only what is absolutely necessary for the good of the team.

Where do these rumours start? Who decides to start one of these amazing stories? Some one must decide to stir it.

The 2 p.m., practice is on grass; the footing is not so wet now, the surface having dried up with the wind and sunshine. Eeyore feels fine; he has had a good rest after his hack. Just before lunchtime, Sophie and I went to his stable and caught him napping, lying down with his nose resting on the shavings. I swear he was snoring!

As we pair up with our partners, it becomes apparent that there are quite a few missing. There are now three horses stabled at Windsor, my partner Vanessa, on the black Karim, her friend on the chestnut, and the little mare who was lame yesterday.

This mare is 25 years old and has been a wonderful horse for her owner/rider. Some years previously, the mare fractured her cannon bone in a front leg; she is lucky to be alive. She had given so much to her rider that they saved her and spent months and months healing the leg.

With all the work over the last few days, the little mare has been feeling pain in that leg. To save her from more stress, the rider has decided to keep her at Windsor to avoid the long hack from Frogmore. It is one and a half hours to ride there and back, which would certainly put strain on her leg. It is a pity that she may not make the show because, at her age, this could be her swan song; a fitting note to end a generous and fulfilling career.

The missing horses make the ride very odd. I have no partner so I am on my own. The little mare is usually in front of me, so I have no horse directly in front of me either. Claire on George partners the little mare so she is in front to my left.

The chestnut normally in front of the little mare has gone to the front, to be the new leader. The original leader should be in her place but there is no sign of her yet.

I have only one horse behind me because Vanessa's friend is also at Windsor. He usually partners the gentleman on the chestnut, the horse who rears in front of the audience.

So we have pairs right up to fourth place, then we have a single rider, followed by another single rider followed by me as a single rider followed by another single rider, then two pairs at the back. This is going to look strange.

Despite that, Eeyore performs beautifully doing what he needs to do. It may have been the hack and the sleep that revived him. Perhaps it is also the weather, though still cool, the sun is shining; everyone appears to be in a better mood.

I am glad because riding in front of Jennie Loriston-Clarke is not just spine-tinglingly scary it is also a tremendous privilege. So I try my best from the start of the practice, sitting as quietly as possible whilst giving the aids in a subtle way.

After the practice, we line up and Jennie walks in front of us giving us her comments. She is like a sergeant major parading the troops, giving her staccato comments.

'You did alright.'

'You need to keep up with your partner.'

'You were good.'

'You were slow at everything. You were late on the circles and turns. Keep up.'

'You did well.'

'You need to sit up straight in the half-pass. Don't lean.'

She arrives in front of Eeyore and me. She pauses for a moment's thought; trying to recollect how we did, here it comes!

'Yes, you were good.' She states and points at us. I am relieved and thrilled at the same time. If I do nothing else it has been worth it for those few words from Jennie.

She continues to the end of the line. The rearing chestnut has performed impeccably today, true to unpredictable form, if that is possible.

Jennie stands and looks at us. She has one unenviable job to do. It seems that the little mare will not be performing tonight because she is still lame. It has been decided that having an odd number, as we did last night, does not work. It does look strange having one horse on its own at the back. One horse will have to drop out.

We all look at each other wondering who she will choose, unless someone volunteers. Should I? I am so close to saying I'll stay out tonight, give Eeyore a rest. But it sticks in my throat. I do want to ride tonight just to prove to myself that I can do it.

Bit like remounting a horse after a fall, it should be done straight away. It is always ten times more difficult after losing confidence, to ride a horse later.

Then Jennie states, 'Tonight Claire with George will go out.'

She chooses the mare's partner, which is regrettably the bay horse George. Such a pity as he is rock steady. If the mare is still off tomorrow though, someone else will be asked to step down. Jennie wants to give everyone a chance to ride for at least one night of the four.

The practice finishes on that note and we make our way back to the stables. Eeyore can have a rest for a couple of hours before we have to start preparing him for tonight.

For an hour, Sophie and I do manage a rest, which really helps. All that soreness is gone, my stomach is back to normal, I even feel hungry and have some soup and bread. It feels like I have not

The Art of Dressage

Dressage is such an amazing sport. I need to sit with balance in the centre of the saddle with all the muscles 'soft' and relaxed but not floppy. I need to feel Eeyore's muscles beneath the saddle so that I can influence them with slight movements of the hips.

My thighs need to be soft against the saddle, any gripping, even the slightest, and Eeyore stiffens and resists. One of my colleagues once described riding as 'controlled relaxation', it is the most difficult poise to achieve. Yet when it is achieved and the horse is moving sublimely beneath me, coming into my hands with softness and submission, I am simply in paradise!

One of the key elements in riding is suppleness from both rider and horse; both can become stiff and rigid through the back. To help the horse become more supple, correctly riding the corners of a school is vital. A horse should be ridden into the corners as deeply as possible, though horses, especially older ones, will begin stiff and should be allowed time to bend through the corners. I ride Eeyore as deep as possible to begin with, and sometimes it is necessary to be quite firm with him. Then as the time progresses I ask for more bend and a deeper corner. This helps him to bend through his back.

A corner should be ridden with the horse bending through the curve. No horse or rider should ever 'lean' through a corner, as if riding a motorcycle. The horse needs to bend through its body. If the horse does have a tendency to lean, the rider can sit up straight putting a little more weight into the outside stirrup to balance the horse, ask for bend by subtle use of the inside rein whilst giving slightly with the outside rein.

After every corner I retake the outside rein and push Eeyore into this contact with my inside leg. Then I ride into the shoulder fore position up the long side of the school, this also helps me to ride the next corner.

Also vital is that communication between horse and rider known as the 'half-halt'. This is a co-ordination of aids that is used prior to any change of direction, pace or movement, transition or even before every corner in the school. It is said that a rider can give up to 400 half-halts in a one hour schooling session!

The half-halt is used to rebalance the horse, making him step onto his hindquarters and use his hind legs more actively. Horses do have a tendency, even highly trained horses, to come 'on to the forehand', when they use the power of their shoulders to move rather than the power of their hindquarters. The horse then feels 'heavy' in the hand and gives the impression of riding 'downhill'.

I use the half-halts frequently by straightening and strengthening my back muscles, putting a little more weight into the saddle. Then by squeezing the outside rein with my hand I send a signal of slight resistance to the horse. Just as he slows down, and this is literally a hair's breadth of slowness, most spectators may not even notice, I use my legs to send the horse onwards. This helps the horse to regain his balance, to slow the pace but maintain the energy.

Riding the half-halt does need practice and experimentation. Each horse needs a different strength of half-halt. With some horses it is better to think of coming to halt from walk, to walk from trot and to trot from canter just for a brief second and then on.

eaten for days! I have more energy now and feel optimistic.
What a difference twenty four hours can make!

Dress Rehearsal means plaiting Eeyore's mane and tail, and
dressing me up in my posh togs. Sophie is unfortunately leaving
me for this evening.   She wants to watch the whole Dress
Rehearsal from the auditorium.

As participant and groom, we were given two free tickets each for
the Dress Rehearsal. Derek is coming, as is my youngest Helena
and my friend Sarah. Sophie kept one of her tickets for herself.
She wants to watch the show the whole way through. She does
not see much of the show from the sidelines, after cycling up after
me, so I cannot blame her, though I will miss her dreadfully
tonight. She has arranged to meet the family at 6.30 p.m., at the
Farm gate on their way into Windsor.

After our rest, we spend most of the afternoon with Eeyore. First
we take him for a walk down the field where he can eat that rich
clover grass. Down goes his head, and he greedily fills his mouth
and rips the grass by moving his head rapidly from side to side.
Sophie and I relax, the sun is out and the air is warmer now.

Then we see a policeman walking towards us. He shouts out and
waves his hand. Sophie and I quickly look around to catch sight
of the person he is hailing. There is nobody about. For one quick
second I feel guilty.   Strange how, even though I have done
nothing to be guilty about, there are certain figures in authority
that make me feel I have done something wrong. Teachers have
that effect too.

'Who does he want?' I ask Sophie quickly as this tall, six footer
strides towards us purposely.

Sophie shakes her head, she looks as worried as I.

'Hi,' the policeman states, grinning from ear to ear. 'For one moment there, I thought you had my 'orse.' He speaks with a northern accent; he looks quite jolly and friendly.

I laugh, 'No, sorry, this is mine.'

'It is amazing, your 'orse is the spittin' image of mine. Except....' he takes a closer look. 'Yours 'as got a white left hind and mine's on 'is right.'

'Which scene are you in?' I ask, I am eager to know our fellow participants.

'Oh we're in Act Eleven. And you?'

We explain about the dressage group, the Highland scene.

'What's your horse?' I ask.

'Oh he's t'big fella. 'is name's Bruno, but 'e's eighteen hands so 'e gets called Big Frank!.' We all laugh at that. 'Actually 'e's in two Acts 'cos a policeman from New York is borrowing 'im for't show.'

Apparently, the New York Police could not bring their horses across, possibly for economic reasons, so they are borrowing these gallant horses from the British Mounted Police. It is lovely to know how this show has brought so many people together and what friendship and generosity there is between ordinary people from all over the world.

After some further conversation, the policeman shakes our hands and leaves.

'Could a sworn twere my 'orse.' He says laughing as he strolls away.

After 'Big Frank's look alike' has had a fair amount of grass, it is time to groom him, clean his feet, oil them and do the plaiting whilst he is tied up outside the horsebox.

Sophie wants to experiment with plaiting his tail. I am supposed to be plaiting his mane, but my fingers feel like a bunch of bananas and I cannot do a thing with them.

I hate to admit it but I persuade my neighbour's groom, Richard, to plait Eeyore. He plaits him beautifully in an hour. Plaiting the mane makes such a difference to the appearance of a horse. Normally there will be about ten or eleven plaits in a mane and one for the forelock; this makes the neck look slightly shorter and thicker.

A greater number of smaller plaits, anything up to twenty-five or thirty, makes the neck look longer and slightly slimmer. The plaits are usually fastened with elastic bands, but they can be sewn with needle and thread. White insulating tape is then wrapped around each plait to make them stand out. This looks beautiful on a dark horse.

Sophie's tail plait is superb, even Richard states that it looks professional. She beams with pride. We spray hair lacquer onto the mane and tail plaits to hold them in. Then putting a tail bandage on the tail to preserve Sophie's wonderful plait, we take Eeyore back to his stable for his tea.

At 5.30 p.m., Sophie receives a call on her mobile. Derek is here to collect her at the Farm Gate. He is an hour early! We both panic, how can she leave me now, we still have so much to do. She was expecting to stay for at least another hour.

'I cannot leave you at this point,' she groans.

I am anxious too. It is the dress rehearsal and I will have to do this all on my own. My toe is still extremely painful which makes walking difficult and I am hopeless at tying stocks. This is a piece of cloth tied around the neck on top of the shirt collar. It is a substitute for a tie, but looks neater and prettier. It is the very devil to fasten. There is a complicated motion of putting it round the neck, threading it through a hole, laying it over the shoulders, passing the ends around each other and at that point I usually give up.

I am close to asking Sophie not to go, but that would be unfair. She has been a rock these last few days, actually it feels like years, since Sunday!

'Go on Sophie, don't worry I will be fine.' I feel far from it. She deserves to watch the show and it would be good if at least one of us sees the whole performance.

The only bit of the show that I have seen is the Act following ours. This is the Dream Sequence and, as I am riding around the outside of the Stadium at this point, I have not seen it clearly. There is a grey horse (in appearance white) with a lady rider in a white flowing dress. Her arms are outstretched with cloth draped from them like wings. She controls the horse from her stomach; the reins are attached around her waist. It looks amazing with the horse rearing and pirouetting.

Originally, there was supposed to be smoke in this scene. They wanted the lady and her horse to come through the smoke as she entered the Stadium, but she stated quite flatly that her horse would refuse to go through the smoke and she could not blame him. Other horses included in the Act objected to the smoke too, so the scene progressed smokeless.

Sophie departs at 6 p.m., and I am on my own, feeling very alone. If I had not given up smoking a year ago I would now be tempted to have a smoke and drink lots of alcohol. I make myself a cup of tea instead, the British thing to do! When in doubt, get the teapot out! It does the trick and calms me down. Tea is a true panacea for all occasions.

12

On my own – panic – text messages!

Our group, Group 1 is scheduled to leave Frogmore at 8.40 p.m., we need to be mounted and ready to go at 8.30 p.m. Five minutes after our departure the Grand Prix riders will depart and Group 2 five minutes after them. The staggered start means that there are only twenty, in our case now sixteen horses, on the hack. This avoids a huge group of almost fifty horses being together. If any of the horses decides to go ballistic, this could set the others off. Safer to have smaller groups in case of incidents.

At 7 p.m., I receive a text message from Sophie. *'Is everything OK? Arrived at Windsor, lots of people here, exciting. Are you OK?'*

'Yes, fine. Am just going to get Eeyore.'

At 7.30 I bring Eeyore from his stable to the horsebox, slowly and carefully, I do not want him to tread on any more toes! I tie him up to some twine attached to a ring on the side of the horsebox and begin to brush him, pick out his feet and give him a haynet to keep him quiet and occupied. He prefers the grass though and starts to eat from the ground. I dress myself in white breeches, shirt, polished boots and spurs.

Another text message from Sophie. *'We are sat in the seats now. We are so proud of you. Is everything OK?'*

'Yes fine, just getting Eeyore ready. C u soon. Mum.'

I tack Eeyore up with the newly cleaned double bridle and the dressage saddle. Dressage saddles are designed with a straighter flap in front, to help the rider's leg stay in position. The girth fastens lower down below the saddle, not under the saddle flap as with normal saddles. This allows the rider's legs to be closer to the horse's sides so that the rider's aids can be subtle but clear.

The dressage horse is taught so many different movements and variations within those movements that the rider's aids need to be precise but light and soft.

Under the saddle each horse is to wear a white saddlecloth, a square piece of material, as opposed to a numnah, which is saddle shaped. To match, each horse will have white bandages on the legs. This provides protection for the horse's legs as well as looking smart.

A text message from Sophie. *'Show starting soon, love you lots. U OK?'*

'Yes fine,' at the moment but I am becoming agitated. It is stock tying time. I have to attempt to put on the stock. My fingers do their usual shape-change into bananas, they become uncontrollable and the stock takes on a life of its own. After ten minutes wrestling in front of the mirror, I shout and yell, and

capitulate. I go next door for help. Michelle kindly and calmly ties the stock and fastens it with a stock pin to my shirt.

I return and put on my pearl earrings, the normal accoutrement for dressage women; make up, hair net and hat, then a pair of white gloves.

Another text message from Sophie, *'It looks wonderful here. Are you OK?'*

Well I would be without all the messages; no, Sophie is only concerned about me.

'Yes, fine. Eeyore and I are nearly ready.'

My mouth is dry, my stomach doing roller coaster type actions, and I need the toilet again, but no time.

At 8.25 p.m., I finish; lock up the box, leave the keys in the grooming kit and prepare to mount.

My mobile phone starts, another message, no time now to look.

Untie Eeyore and bring him around to the horsebox steps, carefully mount. Do not need any accidents now! Check the girth, tight enough, and off we go.

It was a pity that I missed that last message because, as I learn later, it informed me that the seats Sophie and Derek have been allocated are directly in front of where Eeyore and I will be in the Group 1 arena.

All the members of the Dressage Group 1 collect in the horsebox field. We do look smart wearing our outfits. We have been given a sash of Royal Stuart tartan to wrap across our right shoulder down to the left hip. We are part of the Balmoral Scene, the Queen's Scottish residence, which is why we perform to the bagpipes and drums.

The Side-saddle Group is preparing to depart. Although in the same Act, they leave before us because they walk more slowly, their grooms having to accompany them. They look incredibly beautiful in their in black top hats, long specially cut frock coats and a red tartan sash across from shoulder to hip. There is something so graceful about side-saddle.

Others groups have already set off on their long trek, the Polo group, the Mounted Police, the Canadian Mounties, the Coloured Horses, the carriage horses, the 'Cowboys' and the Arabs.

We are supposed to hack with our partners but as my partner is not here, I ride on my own behind the pair in front. This gives me time to look around and appreciate the surroundings. The trimly cut hedges are bordered by carpet smooth grass verges; no wonder the horses are not allowed on these. We ride past the fields with the grazing cows and over the bridges that cross the streams flowing into the Thames. There are soldiers along the route standing sentry ready to offer help if needed and checking that we do not lose our way.

At the cross-country jumping field we pause, waiting for the guns of the Kings Troop. Boom, right on time, boom again and repeat until the rat tat tat at the end. Some of the horses start backing up and rearing, others just ignore it. I jump every time.

We ride under the tunnel at Victoria Bridge, the horses are used to it now and act nonchalant, bit smug really, and up the slight slope of grass to the left. We pass the Side-saddle Group who are waiting on our left. We will meet again in the Chute when they queue up with us.

To our right behind a metal fence there are caravans and tents, more than usual, participants coming for the Windsor Show that is held during the day.

People lean out from the caravans and tents to wish us luck. The atmosphere here already is different, it is charged with anticipation. Children come running to the fence to watch us; couples stop and turn to see us pass. 'Good luck,' they shout and we thank them. Yes, tonight is different. I feel excited but strangely more relaxed. I know the routine now. Eeyore is at ease with the night-time hack and the razzmatazz of the show.

It feels as if we have learnt to trust each other more than we did before. Maybe the walk together in the dark when we went through our worst patch has strengthened the bond. It is often so with humans that they grow closer through adversity, so why not horse and human?

The twilight deepens and as it does so, the lights from the Stadium seem brighter. The sounds are extra loud tonight, with the audience as well, it must be deafening inside there.

Two strobe lights beam upwards, stretching right up into the sky. They shine like twin stars, their lights travelling back in time through the universe. I shiver as a thought passes through me, those lights will shine throughout time, taking this event with them. It will be happening every second throughout the universe. I stare up at the sky, for millions and millions of years this night will be replayed through those lights. I shake my head, thoughts too deep.

It is an amazing event and deserves to go on forever. Consider how much organisation has gone into this and I, I am part of this stupendous happening. To be part of this occasion is a privilege; I am fortunate indeed.

We reach the car park where we waited on Monday night, walking round and round. Monday night, that seems so long ago. Cars and 4 by 4 wheeled vehicles fill this area tonight. We pass more caravans, tents and horseboxes that change the familiar route making it unrecognisable. Here there are crowds, standing and watching. They applaud us as we pass and it makes my heart swell. Eeyore just flicks his ears in response. The back ache, the painful legs, even the swollen broken toe seems to disappear.

Just as we reach the collecting ring, we meet up with the two horses from the Windsor stables. The black who partners me is already on its toes, spinning round and round. How the rider constrains it or manages to keep on amazes me. I feel sorry for her but, at the same time, I am anxious that this does not upset Eeyore again. It is most disturbing when a horse beside you is agitated and nervous; this can affect other horses so quickly.

Once we reach the grass collecting-ring, we group up into pairs and trot around. This settles the horses and helps us to stretch our muscles and joints. The GP riders have arrived too, they are practising their passage and piaffes beside us. It is amazing that we are here side by side amongst some of the top riders of Britain, indeed in the world, as they concentrate rehearsing their movements.

After trotting a few circles on each rein, the man at the opening of the ring tells us now to move forward into the 'Chute'.

There are crowds of people here waiting to see us, they clap and cheer. The black horse next to me spins round and round. It backs into a side-saddle horse; it backs up into Eeyore. I try to persuade Eeyore to move nearer to the crowd, to give Karim some room. Eeyore does not like it though, as several people put their arms through the barrier to stroke him. He jumps away.

'Give that black horse some room,' shouts someone from behind. The horse twists again, crashing once more into the side-saddle horse as the rider tries to kick it on and keep it quiet. I again try to persuade Eeyore to step nearer the crowd. Nice as the horse is and nice as the rider is, I heartily wish it was somewhere else at this moment. What I need now is a quiet relaxed partner to keep Eeyore relaxed as well. Eeyore begins to tense; I can feel him tightening under the saddle. He keeps eyeing Karim, watching him warily.

I feel like yelling, 'Please let us go in, please.' Oh God, if poor Eeyore is wound up again, it will just be the end. Not tonight.

The lone piper starts to play. Thank goodness. Yet we do not move. 'Go in now,' I state loudly. Eeyore is beginning to prance, any minute now and he will explode. He swings his hindquarters round towards the crowd.

Mounted Police preparing for the ride to Windsor.
Girl in foreground going to water tap from stables.

Mounted Police: notice the beautiful cloaks.

Never knew there were so many of them!

'Everyone ready then?'

Collect a group of police persons together and you have a photo shoot, wherever they are! Considering that the old song says that a policeman's lot is not a happy one, all the police at Windsor were a cheerful, happy group!

Right
Police lady in a dress uniform. The uniforms differed widely between divisions.

Left
The famous police horse Bruno, better known as 'Big Frank'.

The Royal Canadian Mounted Police

I can see the leaders start to move! I nudge Eeyore with my legs and we begin to walk forward. Karim settles down and Eeyore slots in beside him as we approach the Stadium.

The atmosphere feels so different tonight; the presence of thousands of people is tangible. The air in the Stadium is a silvery blue, faint smoke clouds drift, lit by strobe lights. The brightness of the floodlights hit us as we turn the corner; the applause is like walking into a physical wall.

The whole world is encompassed by a Lion and a Unicorn, an orchestra, a choir, bagpipers and drummers, and an audience of thousands. The sky is ink black above us; we exist in a bright, thousand bulb strong light.

We are passing the barrier to our right, shadowed faces push forward to see us, hands clap and voices cheer. It is an alien world, peopled by strange pale beings, and we are the focus of their lives.

Eeyore starts to relax as we begin to trot. I push his nose right into the bottom of the horse in front giving him no chance to think about the noise rising to our right.

We trot down to the front of the Stadium bathed in light. In front of us, beyond the curtain of light is a dark shadowed place where pale circles of flesh peer out. They are unknown and nameless, featureless and beyond recognition, their camera flashes spark like blue stars in a misted night sky.

We turn across the Stadium and trot to our arena, our 20 x 60 metres of sand marked out with the four potted bushes, one at each corner.

As we enter our arena, I see something on the floor. It is a sock, a brown sock, looking like a snake in the sand. The type of thing that Eeyore can shy at; I feel myself tighten, gripping with my knees, anticipating his step to the side. He passes it; totally ignores it; he does not even seem to see it! This just might work. I relax.

We trot in pairs down the centre line, around the top end of the school together to the left, as the introductory music is still playing. The bagpipe music starts on cue and we begin our drill.

Everything goes well, we perform the circles and turns, not perfectly it is true but better than we have previously. Eeyore does his shoulder-in, circles and half-passes so obediently. We trot around to the left into the sight of those Scottish dancers, now lit by spotlights; he takes one look and ignores them.

We make the transition to canter; Eeyore feels very enthusiastic. He starts to pull a little, becoming strong in the hand and forward bounding. He is enjoying this; his pace becomes bouncier as he begins to show off. I hold on tightly, strengthening the muscles of my stomach and back to hold him.

The drill is for the group to split into two smaller groups of ten, each of which canters two circles separately. Our group canters the circles to the right; our partners in the other group canter the circles to the left. After the second circle, we meet up with our partners in the centre of the arena. Our horses do a flying change and we then all canter a circle to the left together in pairs.

Round the first circle in canter, wonderful. He is still strong, but I manage to keep him close to the horse in front, his nose almost touching the chestnut's tail. That was our undoing!

The music is playing, the cameras flashing, the horses cantering. Without warning, the chestnut in front of Eeyore suddenly takes a turn to the left; she should have turned to the right to canter another circle in that direction.

She must have miscounted the circles and thought that now she should change direction and canter to the left. As she asks for a flying change on the centre line, her horse slows down. Eeyore, being ridden close behind, catches up, becomes caught in the slipstream and follows, cantering to the left. He performs a beautiful flying change in the centre of the arena.

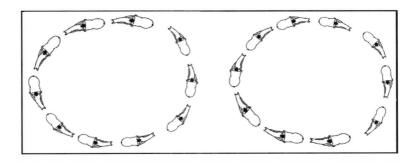

Half the ride canters a circle to the left and we canter a circle to the right

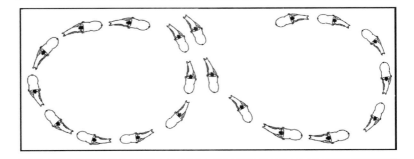

Then we peel off and join the other circle performing a flying change on the centre line

Where are we? I look around; those behind me are going to the right, I turn Eeyore round, ride him on, do another flying change and rejoin the circle slotting back into my place. With any luck, Jennie Loriston-Clarke will not notice this on the video!

As I canter around my second circle I look for my partner to join up with her, only now I notice that the horse in front of my partner, who should have been joined up with the chestnut that went wrong, has no partner. Where did the chestnut go? For the chestnut to miss one canter circle is not disastrous in itself, if she had stayed with her partner, we could all have met our partners the next time around.

Only she does not. For some reason, once she realises she has gone wrong she rides off somewhere else. As I canter round to meet up with my partner, there is no sign of her at all. To this day, I have absolutely no clue as to where she went. She just disappeared.

What do I do? Do I wait for my partner? This will leave the horse in front of my partner on its own; this will appear odd. Or do I join the other horse in front and leave my partner to the rider behind me, hoping they realise what is going on?

I make the decision; I join the horse in front and hope that those behind me change partners. Thankfully, they are clever and do so; catastrophe is averted.

The ride progresses well, once that little hiccup is over. Eeyore performs beautifully, doing his flying changes with a spring; it feels like flying. I giggle; he has that effect on me.

The drill ends with us performing shoulder-in across the top of the school and then forward in trot to the centre line and halt.

Bang - immediately up goes the chestnut that reared last night; it rears and rears again. This time it also lashes out with its front hooves. How the guy stays on is beyond me.

The horse to the side of the chestnut becomes restless, it backs up into the horse beside it and there is a 'knock-on' domino effect. Eeyore starts to become restless too, he moves about, especially when the horse next to him sidles into him. We salute quickly and move off.

I am pleased with Eeyore's performance; even with the horse in front going wrong, he coped. It is a bit disconcerting that it always seems to be the horse in front of us that goes wrong. Am I jinxed? (Watching the video later we never did discover where the chestnut went after it cantered the wrong circle. It is a mystery.)

We trot out of the Stadium and into the night, breathing huge sighs of relief.   It was not correct but it is improving every evening. Perhaps by Saturday we will have it perfect!

Tonight I will hack home; I will not stay for the Finale. I feel relieved, calm, relaxed; I am even enjoying it.   The hack to Frogmore is pleasant. I chat to another rider all the way home, discussing the evening and the whole celebration.

The evening is balmy; the night has gone well as far as I am concerned, at last I feel I can breathe again. I laugh too when I discover that the grey horse accompanying Eeyore on the hack, is called Ivor (pronounced Eevor). Eevor and Eeyore, it was one of those nights. We laugh and laugh, feels like the first time in ages that I have laughed. I feel so much better.

When I arrive back at the stables, my family and friend Sarah are already there. They must have missed the Finale and raced back from Windsor. I wave at them as I enter the field of the temporary stables. I was not prepared for what happened next.

As I dismount, Sophie runs up to me and hugs me so tightly. She is crying!! Crying her eyes out, sobbing. What has happened? Has someone died? I look around; all of them are crying, tears are streaming down their cheeks. It must be serious. Even Derek, who is not prone to emotions of any kind, even he is weeping.

I am stunned. 'What's happened?' I ask anxiously.

Sophie is now crying unashamedly. Helena grabs me round the waist. Sarah is smiling and crying at the same time, her eyes bright, she is unable to speak. Derek is beaming and grabs hold of Sophie, Helena and me together in a group hug. I am still confused and extremely worried.

'We are so proud of you,' Sophie says at last. They all nod their heads; they are overcome with emotion. I cannot believe it.

'I was just so nervous for you,' Sophie whispers and her voice sounds shaky. 'I felt so sick just before your Act.' Sophie hugs me again as she repeats. 'We are so proud of you.'

Helena squeezes my waist tightly and looks up at me, 'Mum it was wonderful. You and Eeyore were wonderful.'

'It was stupendous,' states Derek. My goodness, that is a statement from him. He is a Black Country Lad and they do not give compliments away for nothing, if anything he usually finds a balloon-bursting thing to say. If there is a way to take the wind out of my sail, he'll find it. He is not horsey either so, to stir up this much emotion in him it must have been good, it must have been brain shatteringly wonderful.

Sophie hugs Eeyore, 'He looked so good, Mum. What a star he is. I am so proud of him.'

All the attention now turns to Eeyore. He receives strokes, kisses, hugs and polo mints. Even Derek strokes his neck and gives him a sugar lump. I am rocked into silence. I have never ever seen my family so overcome with emotion.

Eeyore looks completely unabashed by all the adoration; he takes it as his divine right.

'Was it really that good?' I ask. I am completely taken aback by their attitude; I did not expect anything like this.

'It was seeing you in there doing it.' Derek explains. 'Especially as we know what you have been through to achieve this. Well done.'

Sarah comes over to me shyly. 'The whole show was just amazing,' she says, 'and then when you came in, to know someone taking part in it, it brought a lump to my throat.' She stops suddenly, a crack in her voice.

'You were just so good together.' Sophie is positively blubbing now. Helena is beaming amongst her tears. Derek has a shine in his eyes and Sarah is stunned into silence, which if you know my friend Sarah is a wonder in itself.

I am completely overwhelmed. Perhaps what we went through is worth it all, and it is only Dress Rehearsal night.

Between the cries, 'ooh that was wonderful, Eeyore was so good,' all of them singing his praises, we finally put Eeyore back in his stable, give him a midnight feed, hay, change his water, pick out his feet and gently brush him down.

'You go up to the horsebox and put the kettle on,' I tell them. 'I'll follow in a minute.' They all nod at me, turn to go and wander off in front of the stables back to the horsebox.

I just want a minute or two with Eeyore. I turn to him and he gently snorts at me. As I enter his stable and stroke him, he sniffs me with his soft nostrils, blowing air on me. I put my forehead on his neck and he stretches his head round to me, breathing over me with his warm, sweet breath. We have one of those special horse-person moments that are so intimate and so immensely pleasurable. It is a spot of paradise on earth. I feel my eyes stinging. To have the friendship and companionship of this wonderful animal, it is worth being born and living a life.

'Thank you Eeyore,' I speak to him gently. He nudges me, asking for a titbit, so I offer him a sugar lump. He gently wraps his lips around the white cube on my palm and softly lifts it into his mouth.

As I close the stable door, he looks at me with his kind brown eyes and I smile at him. 'I love you Eeyore.' He nods in agreement and then carries on eating his feed.

13

Wednesday 15th May
Day 4 The Aftermath

The night's tales – humour - relief

My family have some amazing tales to tell of the night's performance. It seems things went wrong for quite a few of the acts, embarrassingly so for the professional cavalry!

Sitting down in the horsebox with a cup of coffee, they relate their tales to me.

One poor rider of the Household Cavalry Mounted Band fell off his horse just as he was entering the ring! Having been waiting around to enter for some time, his horse became fractious, spun round extremely quickly and unseated the rider. The poor cavalryman was covered with sand and had to be brushed down by attendants before remounting and entering the Stadium.

More embarrassing perhaps was the fate of the Captain in charge of one of the cavalry regiments (I do not want to embarrass anyone involved by naming the regiment). As part of his act, he had to dismount and stand by the guns as they fired. It was his job to stand there and shout 'Fire, fire, fire!' for each salvo.

Another mounted rider of the troop held the Captain's horse during the time he was issuing the orders. After the guns had discharged, the Captain was supposed to remount his horse.

The horse had other ideas. As the Captain prepared to mount, the horse decided to rear. Up it went, straight up in the air. The Captain must have mounted this horse thousands of times, but the horse had to choose this moment to rear. The Captain could not remount.

Worse than that, the horse rearing set off the other horse, the one ridden by the soldier holding the Captain's horse. That reared too and off came the other member of the troop. There are now two members of the cavalry on the deck.

Using his wit, the trooper decided to help his Captain remount by giving him a leg up. This would have worked had the horse been co-operative. It was not. Horses being horses are born with a supreme sense of mischief; the Captain's horse refused to stand still. It moved and bucked, it twisted round, making it impossible for the Captain to mount. The Captain hopped around desperately, his leg being held by the trooper, trying in vain to mount a moving target, 16 hands of active horseflesh.

By this time, the audience were fully aware of the problems; the sound of suppressed tittering filled the air. The Captain and his attendant cavalry officer were becoming desperate.

It is rumoured, and it is only a rumour, that in the end the officer giving the leg up put his hand on the Captain's seat to push him physically into the saddle. He must have touched a tender spot because the Captain shot up off the ground like a rocket firework!

Another officer in the Household Cavalry had to take out his sword, hold it up front of his face and at a prearranged time to synchronise with all the other officers who were to do the same with their swords, slip it efficiently back into its scabbard. He had to do this whilst keeping his eyes to the front and without looking at the scabbard.

Now whether the scabbard took on a life of its own, or the sword just decided it wanted to stay out longer, the poor officer could not get the sword back into its case. He searched around with the tip of the sword trying desperately to find the scabbard and then once found the sword simply refused to enter. It stuck; it reverberated and recoiled. The other officers waited patiently, swords at the ready. As time went on it became apparent that the sword and scabbard were like two opposing magnets; 'ne'er the twain would meet'.

Eventually the poor chap had to look down, grab hold of the scabbard physically and forcibly drive the sword home. Seems that not only living creatures can be awkward at times!

One of the hounds belonging to the hunting group was lost. It ran off through the fence barrier dividing the Stadium from the seating and into the audience. One of the huntsmen had to climb the barrier and retrieve it. There is also a rumour that one of the hounds urinated on a potted plant, but this is just a rumour!

The Gold Coach too caused problems.

At the end of the Finale, before the horses and participants exit, the plan is that the Coach leaves its protective tent and is pulled by eight Windsor Grey horses at a slow walk around the Stadium before being returned to its marquee.

Tonight the coach became stuck. With its wheels firmly embedded in the sand, this four tons of golden splendour could not be reversed into the marquee.

At first a handful of men were conscripted into pushing it towards the marquee. To no avail. More were volunteered; grunting and groaning they gallantly pushed; muscles straining, brows sweating. More volunteers arrived and with heaving chests and bulging biceps they tried to manhandle this gold covered vehicle, weighing as much as an elephant, into its allotted spot.

The horses, ponies, handlers and riders of the Finale waited patiently in the Stadium as increasing numbers of men, like tiny ants around a massive object, pushed and pulled this astronomically heavy coach stuck imperviously in the sand. As the time passed though, so the horses and riders became restless and impatient. Standing around after a night's work, hours of hacking, performing and waiting in the wings, had not improved the horses' and riders' resilience.

Eventually to the relief of all, especially the event organisers, the huge Gold Coach lost its battle against so much manpower and it slowly began to move, reversing back into its original spot.

So perhaps Eeyore and I taking the wrong route for a few seconds is not the disaster it seems!

14

*More autopsies – heat and sunshine – rest and shopping
the Princess Royal*

As far as the weather is concerned without doubt, this is the best day; very hot sunshine and blue skies, no wind.

My legs are aching from all the riding and my body is beginning to wilt because of the adrenalin. There comes a time when the adrenalin rush finally starts to ease off and the body feels tired. I ask Sophie if she would like to hack Eeyore in the company of Lynn on Isaac and Bev on Bugsy.

Sophie needs only the slightest excuse to ride Eeyore. She adores him. If he was a man I would definitely think there was something going on. She strokes him and pets him and, though she is looking for a horse of her own, nothing is ever going to replace Eeyore.   She wants another Eeyore but unfortunately, horses like him do not grow on trees.

It was only luck that I found him, or perhaps it was fate, kismet or karma.

I owned a young Danish Warmblood, Rufus, who was quite a difficult horse to train.   Some people love training young horses and will constantly buy 3 or 4 year olds, train them for two or three years and then sell them off. After Rufus I realised this was not for me.

One day, whilst walking through the livery yard where I kept him, I was musing on how wonderful it would be to have a trained, educated horse that could teach me; the sort of horse that could do all the 'fancy' bits.

'Funny you should say that,' stated Claire, the yard owner, who was grooming a horse at the time. 'There just happens to be a jet-black Hanoverian for sale, Prix St. George.' My favourite colour, my favourite breed and Prix St. George, give me a break, these horses cost £25,000. No way do I have anything like that amount of money.

'He is 12 years old, the lady who is selling him would prefer he went to a home where he will be looked after, not such a competitive home.'

I decided to check him out, nothing to lose.

The minute I entered Eeyore's box I was smitten. He looked at me, pointing those lovely ears and I was hooked!!!! Then when I saw him being ridden, my tongue hung out. To own a horse like that was my dream. All my life, since the age of nine have I dreamt of owning and riding a horse like this. I have every video of the World Dressage Championships to Music held annually at places with strange names like s'Hertogenbosch and Aarhus. I drool at these horses, I sigh with unrequited love when I see them.

I dream of them and wake up knowing that never in the world would I ever have the chance of owning one. And yet here he is.

Not so much money as I thought. The lady selling him is in favour of me buying him and, after haggling, will bring the price down quite dramatically. Still out of my pocket though. Yet I must have him. How?

I scrape every penny I have together but it is still short. I beg, steal and borrow but my family is not rich and the money is not quite enough. I have a decision to make. I cannot sell Rufus quickly enough to buy Eeyore and there are other people looking at Eeyore, who may buy him. So I sell the car, I can make do with a cheaper one anyway.

Within a few weeks Eeyore is mine. I have never looked back. It was the best decision I made. Rufus was sold a few months later going to a wonderful family who were going to jump and event him. He was bored with dressage.

Horses are like that; some of them prefer to jump. Schooling and flatwork, going round and round a sand arena bores them. Others, like Eeyore, thrive on dressage; the more they do the more they enjoy it. Naturally, not all horses conform to the mould, some good jumping horses make good dressage horses and vice versa.

At Frogmore today no hacking is allowed outside the compound because the horse show at Windsor has started; some of the competitions, such as cross-country carriage driving, take place along the track. We have to ride around the huge field instead, the one in which we did our first practice. It is a beautiful day and Sophie enjoys her ride on Eeyore, she beams with joy whenever she sits on his back.

I leave her to enjoy her ride with Bev and Lynn whilst I muck out and prepare Eeyore's stable for him.

As the morning progresses, the rumours start. They become wilder and wilder, more numerous and intense. There are going to be changes in the groups, changes in the routine, people are dropping out, people are being told to leave. There are going to be more and more practices.

I ignore these rumours. No one in their right mind is going to change anything at this point unless absolutely essential.

Towards lunchtime we are called to Jennie's horsebox for another discussion. As Jennie is competing at Windsor and has little time to spare, Jane Bredin, another of the top Grand Prix riders, gives us our 'pep-talk' for today.

Jane is sympathetic, knowledgeable and understanding. She states that Jennie is aware of the parts of the routine that went wrong last night. We have to put that behind us now and concentrate on tonight. Tonight is the 'real' event, the Princess Royal is attending; we do need to ride as correctly as possible.

Jane Bredin and Jennie Loriston Clarke are both at the top of their profession yet they have given their time and energy to help coach us for this occasion. Often it seems to be the case that those truly at the top of their profession do not have an attitude problem, they are willing to help us lower ranks, passing on their knowledge and expertise.

We give Eeyore his lunch at 12.30 and settle him down for the afternoon. No practices today as yet, it seems the rumours are incorrect.

We have arranged to meet Derek, Helena, Martyn my son, Rhoda and Ian my friends at the gate at 1.30 p.m., to go to Windsor Horse Show. Sophie and I need to do some serious shopping!!!

We meet at the Farm Gate and Martyn gives me a huge hug. This is unusual for my six foot, seventeen year old boy, hugging mother is so uncool. He says he has missed me so much. I have only been away five days! Perhaps it feels more for him as well.

The Royal Windsor Horse Show is a grand event; many, many shops and stalls selling lots of goodies. Horse tack shops, clothes shops, books and gifts, souvenirs, riding gear, dresses, evening wear, dinner suits, leather boots and shoes, handbags and accessories. Masses of things to buy even for non-horsey people. One shop even had three little alpacas in an enclosure to advertise their alpaca wool clothes. What gorgeous animals they are.

At the same time there are competitions going on, riders on horses are jumping massive fences. I am awed by the size of the fences; they are huge, at least five foot and that looks big from the ground.

The Show at Windsor was inaugurated in 1943 and both the Queen, then Princess Elizabeth, and her sister Princess Margaret competed in that first year in a driving competition. Prince Philip has also competed many times at Windsor in driving competitions.

The sun is beating down on us, what a beautiful day. Walking around the stalls and competition rings though makes me feel quite tired. It has been a long week for Sophie and me. My toe is throbbing and, being pressed against the side of my shoe, feels sore. I am also apprehensive about tonight and anxious about leaving Eeyore on his own at Frogmore.

We return to the stables at 4.30 p.m. Though I miss my family, I am glad to be back. It feels like coming 'home'. Eeyore is fine, resting in his stable. He is glad of his feed and Sophie and I retire to the box where we have a short nap.

Group 1 meets at the usual time of 8.30 p.m., to depart at 8.40 p.m. The hack is extremely pleasant tonight, warm and quiet.

The horses are now so relaxed with their ride to Windsor, as if they have done this all their lives. No more do we suffer the stress of Victoria Bridge, most of them are even becoming accustomed to those King's Troop guns exploding. These are loud enough here a mile away; the noise of those guns has to be ear splitting in the Stadium.

Unfortunately, when we arrive at Windsor and meet up with Karim, he is still a neurotic, nervous wreck. He spins around, backs off, prances; thank goodness Eeyore seems to be coping with it now.

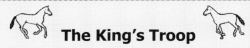

The King's Troop

The King's Troop Royal Horse Artillery is part of the Household Troops and dates back to around 1800.

This Troop so impressed King George VI that in 1947, he renamed the regiment the King's Troop and Queen Elizabeth decided to keep this title in memory of her father.

Stationed at St. Johns Wood in London their duties include firing royal salutes in Hyde Park, at royal anniversaries, and providing gun carriages with teams of black horses for State and Military funerals. When on parade the King's Troop takes precedence over other regiments. As part of their duties too, they perform their spectacular drill all over the world. At each show they use around a hundred horses, a hundred men and six guns. Audiences really appreciate their courage and precision.

At one point the teams gallop flat out with six horses pulling guns on carriages weighing one and a half tons and they do this whilst performing the scissors, with teams crossing each other in the centre of the Stadium.

Then they face each other, three teams either side and race directly at each other fitting precisely into the spaces between horses and carriages.

What makes the sight more impressive are the wonderful uniforms, the plumed hats and the flashing swords. The highlight of the performance is their exit; they leave at a frantic full gallop, the horses' hooves sending sand flying. The sight is breathtaking.

We wait in the Chute until our cue and enter to the lone piper. We ride our entry into the Stadium, down the right hand side, through the cheers, shouts of joy, hurrahs and applause. The horses merely twitch their ears, they are becoming accustomed to the noise and atmosphere.

We trot across the Stadium, in front of the royal podium, to our arena.

As we enter the arena, down the centre line at 'A', the rider on Karim whispers urgently to me 'Oh God, there are things in the arena.'

'Where?' I ask not daring to look around.

'On the floor,' she answers.

'Don't worry about them. There was a sock yesterday and they just rode over it,' I explain, thinking there are similar objects left by a previous Act.

'No,' she urgently insists. 'There are bushes in pots all down the centre line!'

She is right, as we ride onto the centre line, there, beautifully spaced out in a long line, are bushes in pots, four of them. How are we going to perform the movements, the circles, the turns, the half-passes, all of which depend on the centre line? How are we going to avoid hitting them? A horse could trip over them or at least shy and spook?

Riding in pairs, it is difficult to miss objects placed on the centre line. Why should anyone place pots on the centre line? It is a rider's nightmare!

Do we go to one side together or ride either side of the pots? We decide to ride together on one side of the pots. For the circles and turns we judge it so that we narrowly miss hitting the obstacles, for the half-passes we manage to ride between the pots, in the canter circles we go round them. Those pots certainly keep our minds focused on the routine.

It does not help that the little mare in front, recovered from her lameness and back in our group, is obviously feeling well as she canters around the whole routine. She refuses to trot. How she misses the pots is a mystery. She is a gallant little soul and, as her rider is competent, she keeps her under control.

Eeyore seems to be settling into the routine and I am more accustomed to it myself. Although he becomes quite strong and I feel almost at the point of losing control, when I strengthen my back muscles and squeeze the reins, asking him to listen to me, he does.

We ride the trot half-passes, the circles and turns, skilfully manoeuvring around those pots. We begin the canter, ride through the canter circles and the flying change before we begin our canter half-passes. We perform the first canter half-pass to the left beautifully. We canter along the top of the arena, turn right towards the audience and prepare to canter half pass to the right after the next corner, when it happens.

Suddenly, the chestnut, two pairs in front of us, stops dead! Then he reverses at speed and smacks directly into the horse behind. The backward motion throws his rider forward with the momentum; she lands heavily on his neck losing control.

Even half a ton of horse can stop on an instant when it wants. It can spin on the spot and shoot off before the rider has time to breathe, causing problems for those directly behind who do not have the time to avoid trouble.

It is the rock solid George who is involved this time. The chestnut's bum drives straight into his chest. No matter how rock solid a horse is, this will have an effect.

George is stunned for a second, stops from the impact and loses his concentration. The little mare, his partner proceeds forward for a few steps then stops as she realises her partner is not there. The chestnut has veered off to the side now so with quick thinking George's rider Claire, together with the little mare's rider Paula, urge their horses on and continue by sidling around the chestnut.

I breathe a sigh of relief, offer a prayer of thanks to whoever is in charge for being one place removed this time; Eeyore and I are not directly involved. We have the time to ride around the static chestnut horse and continue the routine.

All too soon we are trotting around the three loop serpentine. We ride up the short side to the top; perform our shoulder-in along the top side; then, when the leader starts we ride forwards to the 'centre line' and halt.

Instantaneously there is a thunderous applause. It hits us like a huge wave of sound. The shock of it shakes the riders and spooks some of the horses.

It is a strange feeling; we perform our routine, concentrating solely on keeping the horses under control, maintaining the timing of the sequences with our partner, aware only of our immediate vicinity, that we exclude the fact that there is an audience. Then we stop with relief and suddenly are hit with a totally unexpected tidal wave of sound.

There is a full audience tonight, four thousand strong, the atmosphere is charged and the cheering, whooping and yelling is stupendous.

I stare in disbelief; did we perform _that_ well? Emotion is running high within me; I swell with pride and joy. I can understand how entertainers become addicted to this acclaim. It is breathtaking and exhilarating.

Then that chestnut rears; up she goes, straight up on her hind legs. This time she goes so high there is a real threat that the horse will fall over backwards. Eeyore sees it happen and pulls back, hiding behind Karim, who uncharacteristically is standing still!

The applause hits us, carrying on and on. This is all too much for Eeyore, who fidgets, backs up, spins around once. I push him into line again, trying to regain control, but he is on his toes now.

The rider on the chestnut, frightened by his horse's rearing, yells at us to 'Go, go, go.' We cannot wait for the GP riders to halt and salute. The chestnut horse is going loopy and is upsetting those around it.

We push the horses forward towards the crowd. The applause and yelling is still overpowering. We join our partners, turn left and trot down the side of the Stadium to the exit. As we leave, I am quite happy. Eeyore behaved extremely well, for most of the time. He did not spook, stop, or put a foot wrong during the routine. I will though need to be firmer with him in the halt; he must learn to stand still even with the thunder of applause.

Eeyore and I walk all around the perimeter of the Stadium and the auditorium. My partner and her colleague peel off to return to their stables at Windsor; Eeyore and I are left on our own.

As we pass the collecting ring, I look up to my right. There, on the hill, illuminated and looking down on us like some benevolent grandmother stands the beautiful Windsor Castle. I sigh deeply, it is a poignant moment.

As a solid and ancient sentinel, lit now by a soft orange light, it is an amazing backdrop to the whole show. The towers and battlements stand aloof yet seeming part of it all. Detached from the show though it is, it is still an integral part of it.

My thoughts run on as I stare at the castle from my horse's back, it will be here when we are all gone and it will witness other great events. It signifies hope that things will go on no matter what. As I stare at it, taking in its beauty, one of those rare moments happen when time seems to stand still, or at least to move so slowly that its passage is not apparent. Everything reverts to slow motion, life's own action replay. Moments like this spread themselves out so that they are greater than days, weeks, months or years. This gives me the time to ponder, to wonder and to fully live each second of this loop in time.

How fortunate I am to be here, part of this occasion, staring up at a floodlit Windsor Castle. I am here, now, in this precious moment of my life, I want it to last forever, I feel so very proud.

A horse and rider pass by me. Eeyore nods his head; he wants to move onwards. The moment is over and life tumbles back into its own momentum.

 Windsor Castle

This ancient Castle has been a royal residence since Saxon times. Originally built as a motte and bailey by William the Conqueror almost 1,000 years ago, it acted as a defensive position to guard the western approach to London. The castle has been added to and restored since then by various monarchs during the centuries.

Buried here are ten sovereigns including Henry VIII and his third wife Jane Seymour, the only one to have borne him a son. King Charles I, he who was beheaded after the English Civil War, is also buried here.

Windsor Castle, as one of the Queen's royal residences, is the largest occupied castle in the world; in entirety it covers around 13 acres. Parts of the castle were fully restored after that disastrous fire in 1992, ten years ago.

15

Thursday 16th May
Day 5 The Return

Trouble with teeth – friends and family

As I continue the return ride to Frogmore, I catch up for a little while with one of the Grand Prix riders. Their drill ride went disastrously wrong tonight. She is almost in tears; I know just how she feels!

'My horse refused to do an extended trot across the diagonal,' she states. 'It cantered. I feel so stupid.' Perhaps the GP riders are having as hard a time as we are!! A lot of the tension is probably due to fatigue, nerves and anxiety.

Though we are not competing against each other in this event; we are all suffering from weariness and worry trying to do our best in front of our Royal Family.

The Arab Society

Founded in 1918 the Arab Horse Society is a registered charity created to promote the breeding, importation and use of pure-bred Arabian horses, and to encourage introducing Arabian blood into light horse and pony breeding.

The Arabian horse is an elegant, slender hardy horse, with a concave, 'dish' face that can be extremely pretty in appearance. Despite their delicate appearance, Arabian horses are famous for their stamina and are used particularly for endurance riding.

Arab horses are extremely important to many breeds in the British Isles, many native ponies, such as the Welsh have Arab blood in their lines. More significantly perhaps is the fact that the English Thoroughbred is descended from three Arabians brought over in the 17th and 18th Centuries. These horses were the Byerley Turk, the Darley Arabian, and the Godolphin Arabian. Weatherby's Stud Book, which began in 1791, is based on these three Arabians.

Byerley Turk

Captain Robert Byerley, of the Sixth Dragoon Guards under King William III of Orange, captured the horse Byerley Turk from a Turkish officer at the siege of Buda in Hungary in 1688. Captain Byerley brought the horse to England and used him as a warhorse when dispatched to Ireland in 1689. Later in 1690 the horse was used in the Battle of the Boyne. Byerley Turk, an unmarked, dark brown horse, was used at stud in England, at Middridge Grange, County Durham and later at Byerley's Goldsborough Hall, near Knaresborough, in Yorkshire.

Darley Arabian

The Darley Arabian was acquired from the Syrian Desert near Aleppo; he was the property of the Fedan Bedouins. The British Consul, Thomas Darley, noticed the colt and sought to purchase him. The Sheikh of the tribe, however, tried to back out of the contract desiring instead to keep the bay colt for himself. Darley persuaded some sailors to acquire the colt and he was smuggled out of Syria, arriving in England in 1704. He lived until the ripe old age of thirty years.

Godolphin Arabian

The Godolphin Arabian, a reddish bay stallion, was imported from France in 1729 and came into the possession of Francis, the second Earl of Godolphin, whose family house was situated near to the town of Newmarket. During his life, this horse became attached to a cat called Grimalkin. There are paintings that show the Godolphin Arabian with his cat companion.

When the horse died in 1753, at around 29 years of age, another good age for a horse, he was buried under the gateway at the stable and a stone slab laid with an inscription noting who lay there. The grave is still in existence inside the archway of the stable block within the complex inside Wandlebury Rings.

Sophie has biked over tonight and she is waiting for me in front of Victoria Bridge. We walk through that tunnel with no problems at all now. It seems an age ago when we first shot through here. It is amazing how horses can become accustomed to strange circumstances in a relatively short time, yet in contrast can act up at the slightest provocation when least expected. Apparently the Arabs had the brunt of it tonight. According to Sophie who, whilst waiting for me, spoke to some of the horses going home from previous acts it was the Arab horses tonight who spooked, shied with some bolting off across the stadium.

I love Arab horses. Their elegance, with their beautiful dish face and long slender legs, is utterly deceiving as their remarkable endurance and stamina is renowned. I well remember, once on a holiday in Egypt, being so mesmerised by a stunning Arab horse, that I grabbed him, mounted him and rode off around the step pyramid at Saqqara…. Ah but that is another story!

Even Arab horses can be unpredictable at times and it is this sort of unpredictability and the spirit with which riders deal with it that makes this celebration such a special occasion. Events involving cars, bikes, mechanical devices, are difficult enough, but where horses and ponies are involved, we are dealing with living creatures with minds and temperaments of their own.

We may practise a routine until it is almost perfect, but at any time, the horse can decide it is going another way, or doing something different. Instinct can prevail and the horse will act to preserve its safety from a presumed threat.

It is at those moments that the strength of character of both horse and rider, and the relationship between the two, becomes evident. The overcoming of difficulties by courage and determination is what creates the atmosphere at such an occasion as 'All the Queen's Horses'. Human and equine endeavour metamorphose a mere equine event into a sublime phenomenon.

Sublime too it can be, for there are those times when a horse's huge heart gives the rider 110% effort, ability and love. With no other prey animal do we have such a special relationship.

Perhaps this courage and determination at such an occasion is really only a reflection of the relationship between a horse and rider throughout their lives. Eeyore and I did not have it easy from the beginning, far from it.

Little did I know when I purchased him that I was ill; for months after I bought him I felt so tired and weak. I thought the lethargy was the winter months; I do not like cold weather. By spring though it was obvious that something was desperately wrong.

Gradually as the months passed I found it difficult to get out of bed, I had no interest in anything going on around me, which really is not me at all. As this had progressed slowly, I did not realise that the condition had become so bad. Then one day a friend told me in no uncertain terms to go to the Doctor.

Several blood tests later, the result was that I had a kidney dysfunction. My kidneys were excreting all the potassium in my body. Potassium is vital for muscle function, maintenance and development, and is present in the nervous system to the muscles.

My muscles were literally 'wasting away'; no wonder I had no energy, no desire for living.

Bananas, orange juice and a supplement of Chelated Potassium began to heal me and gradually I clawed my way back to health. Takes quite a time though once something like that has affected the muscular system.

Little did I know that Eeyore was not well either.

Some months after I purchased him the yard manager noticed that he was not properly chewing his oats. They were coming out in his droppings whole, almost as they went in!

We contacted the Equine Dentist, who specialises in dentistry for horses. Most horses have their teeth done by the Vet, and though some Vets may be quite knowledgeable, I regret to say that most are not. Bit like visiting your GP to have your teeth done.

The dentist looked in Eeyore's mouth and nearly yelled. There at the back was the most horrifying condition possible, the worst that he had ever seen.

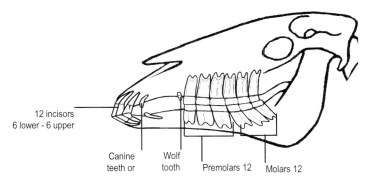

12 incisors
6 lower - 6 upper

Canine
teeth or

Wolf
tooth

Premolars 12

Molars 12

In the adult horse there are 12 incisor teeth at the front and 24 molars or grinding teeth, of which the front three on the top and bottom jaws are termed premolars. All male and some female horses have 4 tushes, or canine teeth between the incisors and molars.

Some horses also have wolf teeth that erupt in front of the premolars. The wolf teeth usually need extracting.

The teeth of a horse are specifically designed for grazing. During the horse's life the root cavities shrink, pushing the teeth out from the gum. This constant 'growth' is balanced by the action of grazing and chewing which wears away the teeth keeping the length constant.

At around the age of 4 years, for some reason, Eeyore's back right molar on the lower jaw was extracted. During the years since, the top molar, having nothing to grind on, emerged from the gum without being worn away.

Proper and regular dentistry would have spotted this problem and dealt with it by rasping the tooth, or even cutting away the excess every year or so. In Eeyore's case the tooth was allowed to grow and grow until eventually it made contact with the jawbone.

After that the tooth began to grind away at the bone until it bore a hole into the bone itself! Eeyore must have been in agony at some points in his career. As the dentist himself stated, 'It shows the good nature of this horse that he was able to rise to such a high standard whilst in such pain.'

When the dentist asked me to look into Eeyore's mouth, it was clear, there was a wall of tooth from the top jaw, digging right into his bottom jaw. It was horrendous. Two operations later and Eeyore is now fine, though he still has the hole in his jawbone.

We both recovered from our ordeals and maybe sometimes, the tougher the road, the stronger we become.

I am so glad of Sophie's company tonight. For some reason, I begin to feel a bit low and lonely. I do not know why I feel this way tonight, I just do. I was on my own on the hack from Frogmore to Windsor because I have no partner with whom to ride. Normally this would not bother me, as I am a bit of a loner. Tonight though I feel it, so I am pleased Sophie is here with me.

We arrive at the stables at around 11 p.m., and begin to prepare Eeyore for his night's rest. My family and friends should visit us tonight if the security will allow them in the Park.

At midnight, we receive a call from Derek. The traffic leaving Windsor is horrendous, only now are they on their way to Frogmore. I am anxious; the gates are locked at midnight. The Frogmore Security does allow them entrance and we meet at Eeyore's stable.

Pride for Eeyore shines in their eyes, how well he looked, how wonderful. Rhoda is brimming with wonder, Ian is quiet but his silence speaks volumes. Martyn insists on giving me huge hugs and cuddles. Must have affected him too, he is, like his dad, usually so stoic and unemotional.

I send them all off to the horsebox to prepare the coffee whilst I have my 'special time' with Eeyore.

After giving Eeyore some sugar lumps, which he takes as his due, I stroke his neck and face. He loves this; it is our petting time. I gently stroke over his eyes, his cheeks, taking time particularly over his mouth and nostrils. This part of his anatomy I think is especially beautiful, soft, dimply and warm.

It is good to give the horse pleasure around this area. We are always placing metal bits in the mouth, clamping the mouth shut with a flash or drop noseband, putting on a curb chain that goes around the chin from the bit in a double bridle. Stroking around a horse's mouth, fondling it, means he has pleasure from our touching this area and it increases the bond between horse and rider.

I stroke Eeyore's poll and his beautiful ears. He goes on munching his hay nonchalantly but I know he is enjoying it because when I stop he gently nudges me with his head for more.

The communication between a horse and rider exists on so many levels. The relationship has an intimacy that we do not experience with any other creature. Stroking him like this, scratching his mane half way down his neck, just as other horses do in the field, makes me part of his herd, not just his 'alpha' Mum, but his friend and companion. With this sort of relationship, a rider/owner should be able to touch every part of their horse without the horse pinning his ears back, baring his teeth or raising a hindleg. There should be a complete trust, being able to touch the horse everywhere without any objections.

I lay my head against his neck and smell his own distinctive smell. I love the scent of him. No doubt, I have a scent too which he recognises. He certainly knows when I am around even before he sees me.   In the mornings before catching sight of me, he whickers softly down his nostrils and puts his head over the stable door looking for me.   I love it when he does that; it is his own special greeting to me.   It is full of love and need and pleasure.   It makes me feel alive and fulfilled.

I put my head once more on his neck and listen to his contented munchings.   It is warm in the stable, full of his breath and body heat.   Then as I turn to go he lifts his head and looks at me.   'Bless you Eeyore,' is all I can say as I give him one last sugar lump.

Words are so inadequate, how can I explain how I feel about this amazing creature.   How much he fills my life, how much he gives to me, how much he teaches me about life and about myself.

16

Friday 17th May
Day 6

The Wessex's – more trials and tribulations

I wake up and am not even sure what day it is, but I know we must do it all again. I imagine working in a circus is like this, one day flowing into another, every day is a new day but every day is the same. It is all so exciting yet so much of a routine.

Weariness is beginning to set in now. Sophie is fast asleep; she seems more tired than I. She is doing the same amount of work, looking after Eeyore, dashing around, bicycling to and from Windsor, but without the adrenalin boost. I leave her to sleep and go to feed and water Eeyore by myself.

The sky is grey today; the wind cold and there is the threat of rain in the air. Later in the morning after Sophie awakes, we take

Eeyore out for a walk in his headcollar and leadrope. How much he loves to graze on the clover rich grass. I muck out his stable and manage to purloin another bale of shavings. This makes the bed more dry and comfortable.

By 10.00 a.m., both Sophie and I are tired and, putting Eeyore back in his stable, we decide to return to the horsebox for a rest. Within five minutes we are both asleep and remain so for two and a half hours until 12.30 p.m. We both feel better for that. Sleep is the restorer of energy and high spirits!

When we go to check on Eeyore at lunchtime, he is flat out in his stable. According to Lynn, who is tending to her horse Isaac next door, Eeyore has been asleep all morning! Seems Sophie and I are not the only ones to need a well deserved rest.

The atmosphere here at Frogmore is now more relaxed, people and horses are settling into the routine. The rushing around trying to find supplies has ceased, as has the racing to rehearsals and practices. Some people are even trying to sunbathe outside their horseboxes, though the sun today appears only fitfully.

Despite that, the rumours still abound. We hear on the grape vine that some of the horses are not going to perform tonight. No-one knows for sure who is 'out' and who is 'in'. Eeyore has performed well but I am still anxious, if there is an odd horse, they may ask me to leave.

Some of the rumours prove true, which is the trouble with rumours, they can never be totally discarded, there is always the possibility of an element of truth in them. Without that, I suppose they would not be as powerful as they are.

One horse to leave is the chestnut who rears on the centre line; the rider has offered to withdraw in the interests of the group. This is so sad as apparently his family will be in the audience tonight. Though he rides the horse well it must have been a fearful moment waiting for her to rear the instant she reached the centre line.

One of the other horses has also gone because the lady rider is competing at Windsor and feels it is too much for her horse to perform at night as well. A couple of horses have also been asked to stand down in Group 2; our ranks grow thinner.

At last Sophie and I have the time to wander about the Barracks area where we are stationed. Sophie, who is armed with her camera, and I decide to have an explore.

We walk down to the temporary stabling to check on Eeyore and, for the first time, to go beyond his stable around the various 'lanes' of this small but crowded temporary 'town'. Rank upon rank of wooden stables stand like rows of soldiers in a company or like those terraced streets in northern English towns. And just as in those northern streets, the inhabitants of the stables poke their heads nosily out of their doorways as we pass. Only these are horses not humans, who look at us pleadingly for titbits, whilst others snort, turn away and resume their hay munching.

In one of the stables there appears to be nothing until we walk directly up to the door. Standing there, no taller than a large dog, is a cream pony. It is so tiny he cannot raise his head above the door; only his pink muzzle sticks out when he wants to see what is going on beyond his stable confines.

Down one of the 'streets' there is a great grey horse tied to one of the stables. His tack includes a special saddlecloth supporting Police insignia. The police are all around laughing and chattering, creating an atmosphere of harmony and fun. Their huge horseboxes surround the stables advertising that they come from all over the United Kingdom. There is a real feeling of camaraderie and friendship. Police on leisure time can be amazingly wild! They certainly know how to enjoy themselves.

Sophie and I continue to walk down to the catering tent. This is an interesting area. We walk through the ornamental gates to find four police persons on their horses posing for pictures. This is just too good an opportunity to miss. The house behind is beautiful but we never did discover what it was or why it was built.

Frogmore is an extremely interesting place and, though I know of it, never have I visited it. It is one of those oddities of life that the nearer you live to somewhere the less you visit it.

At 5 p.m., all the dressage riders, in full dress, assemble on the horsebox field for a photo shoot. It is the first time that all the Dressage Groups have been together, almost fifty of us. Those riders whose horses are at Windsor are here on foot.

Frogmore

There has been a royal residence at Frogmore since around 1680 when the first house was built. George III extended the house in the 1790's for his wife Queen Charlotte who used it as a country retreat for herself and her unmarried daughters, holding receptions and masques in the gardens.

Queen Victoria adopted Frogmore as one of her favourite retreats. It was here that she chose to build the mausoleum for her beloved husband Prince Albert when he died in 1861, though it was not finished until 10 years later. Queen Victoria is buried here beside him.

The Earl Mountbatten of Burma was born in Frogmore House in 1900 and later George V and Queen Mary stayed here with their children from time to time. George VI and Queen Elizabeth spent part of their honeymoon here.

The house now lies in the midst of the private Home Park of Windsor Castle and, though no longer a royal residence, is sometimes used by the Royal Family for official receptions.

Frogmore House, Gardens and Mausoleum are open to the public on a limited number of days each year. Visitors are allowed entrance a couple of times a year during May and August. The mausoleum is open for one day only in May. I must return and visit this spot again sometime.

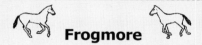

As the professional photographer and a few amateur ones such as Sophie are snapping away at the horses, the weather begins to change. Dark clouds arrive and the wind begins to blow cold. Thunderstorms are forecast for tonight. Great! That's all we need. For tonight we are performing in front of the Earl and Countess of Wessex.

Once more we meet at 8.30 p.m., on the horsebox field but the atmosphere is different. Riders and grooms are chattering and laughing. Instead of that nervous silence of previous evenings, everyone seems so relaxed. We are familiar now with the hack from Frogmore to Windsor and the drill ride that we perform. The horses are acclimatised to the noise, sounds, and smells within the Stadium. It is as if we have been staying at Frogmore and performing the show for weeks instead of two nights!

Though the groups are gelling together now, there are still undercurrents in the teams between various factions – one of the lead file riders is not popular, mainly because her horse keeps stopping or backing off, causing problems. This rider knows she is not popular and is gossiping about the others that are complaining about her. Glad to be out of it, I do not know any of the protagonists so fortunately do not become involved. Politics, it seeps into everything!

Tonight Sophie decides to go by shuttle bus again. She is tired; but when I suggest that she should stay at Frogmore and rest in the box, she refuses emphatically.

'I don't want to miss a second of it,' she states flatly. 'It is only a week, it will all be over soon, then I can rest.'

Then there is Helena, my youngest at 12 years old. She has been angling all week to stay with us in the horsebox. She wants to be a part of the excitement. Stable Management Office agrees to let her stay and she is given a blue wristlet like ours, which allows access to Frogmore and Windsor.

She is so excited to be staying with us. She will sleep in the luton with Sophie; there is plenty of room and Helena is as thin as a stick. There is nothing of her, why the wind does not blow her away, I'll never know.

As we approach the night performance, I begin to look forward to it for the first time. Eeyore looks relaxed and happy. He is becoming an old trooper, really entering the spirit of it all.

Amazing to think that just a short week ago, none of the dressage group knew the drill ride, and only a few of them had even met before. Most of us were strangers to each other, not knowing each other's capabilities or riding skills.

It has been tough learning the routine, learning to work as a whole. Perhaps that is what drew us together as a team. There is a certain camaraderie when people pass through difficult circumstances as though fear, pain and facing overwhelming odds brings them together, melds them into a force. I suppose the saying is we are all in the same boat; if people cannot manage to work together in a boat then there is no chance.

The Dressage Group meet on the field as usual at 8.30 p.m. Timing it exactly right, the weather changes and it begins to rain. The Stable Management office hand out waterproofs for the riders. These waterproofs appear to be nothing more than large clear plastic bags. These rustle and crackle in the wind; some of the horses object to them.

As we line up to depart there is a little surprise for me; someone shouts that I have a new partner, a lady called Ros with another black horse, whose stable name is Hooly.

Ros rides across and introduces herself. I am astonished; this is complete news to me. Her original partner, the rider who is competing at Windsor show, has dropped out. Hooly looks a handsome horse, a Latvian Warmblood and, what is most important, a laid back, quiet type, steady and un-neurotic.

The next surprise is that I have moved up the ride. I was seventh but Ros and her partner were third. I am in third place now, super. It is safer and easier at the front. There are fewer horses in front who are likely to go wrong, spook and bolt, and the speed is slower.

I have a new partner and a new position, third from the front. I am proud; it feels like promotion, though in reality it is not. Yet it proves the best move ever.

It also means that I have a partner to walk and talk with on the hack to Frogmore, which makes me feel more relaxed and wanted. Silly I know, but in these situations, the mind plays funny tricks, it creates wild and imaginative stories! Eeyore seems to like and be happy with Hooly. They are alike in looks and temperament, quiet, steady with just a hint of mischief and spirit.

Eeyore enjoys the company, as do I. Halfway through the ride a shiver passes through my stomach and back, like a premonition, this evening I am going to really, really enjoy it. I relax and let the feeling of joy and excitement flow through me.

Even the downpour that occurs five minutes after we start the ride cannot dampen my spirits. The rain comes down in straight lines and my black jacket is soaked within minutes. It now looks like patent leather.

Waiting in the Chute this evening is positively pleasant, we stand there, still and quiet, no moving, no backing up, no horse spinning round next to me. Hooly is relaxed and steady; what a difference it makes. I can concentrate on the previous Act in the Stadium, listening to the commentary and the music. I see carriages and carts being driven and the commentator is talking about how the Queen has so many carriages.

As we wait in silence I look back behind me along the line to where my original partner is, and yes, there is the horse spinning round and round and round. I breathe a huge sigh of relief.

That night is magic! It is the most wonderful, relaxed, smiling, soft, enthralling evening of them all. As the lone piper plays, we enter the Stadium. The loud applause that hits us like a physical wall is now a more familiar and welcome sound. The bright lights, the music, the audience, we lap it up tonight. Eeyore begins to show off; he flips his toes in the trot. I even hold back a bit with my partner putting some distance between us and the grey horses in front so that Eeyore can show his paces! What a difference. With less horses in the ride too, there is more room for us. Eeyore is in his element; he is bouncy, floating, soft in the mouth, his body language says 'Look at me, aren't I the most handsome horse you have ever seen.' I sit up tall, I feel so proud of him.

Everything goes like clockwork for my partner and I. It is as though we are made for each other, we keep perfect time, meet at exactly the right moment after our circles. It is truly amazing as though everything has just slotted into place.

Eeyore performs his movements with grace and rhythm. The bushes in pots are not placed on the centre line tonight, but there is an orange ball left from the polo Act. Eeyore just ignores it.

I am so relaxed I even listen to the music at last. It is beautiful to enter to the lone piper and to start our drill to a Scots Reel. This always engages the audience who clap in time to the music. As we start to canter the music changes to that haunting melody, 'The Gael' from the 'Last of the Mohicans.' My heart is about to burst; I am loving every minute of it.

At the end of our routine, over all too quickly, Eeyore extends his trot to the finishing line. I can feel the power in his hindquarters launching his body upwards and forwards.

Jennie Loriston-Clarke inspecting her 'troops'

Some of the Grand Prix riders

Members of Group 1 (Top and Bottom), pose for the photo shoot; the riders standing are those whose horses were stabled at Windsor.

Jennie Loriston-Clarke on her stallion Humbug who, incidentally, as well as performing in the evening shows and competing at the Windsor Horse show, was also carrying out his duties as a stud stallion during the week - that horse has stamina!

Checking that everything is just right!

Eeyore II (aka Mr E) a special character

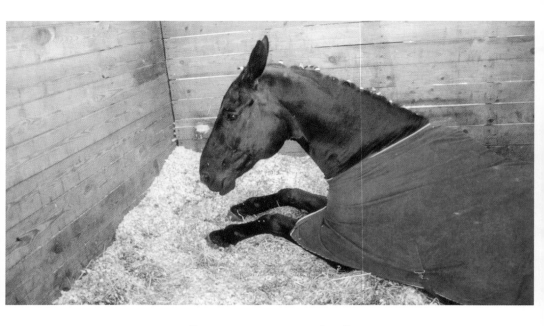

Eeyore was so very tired!

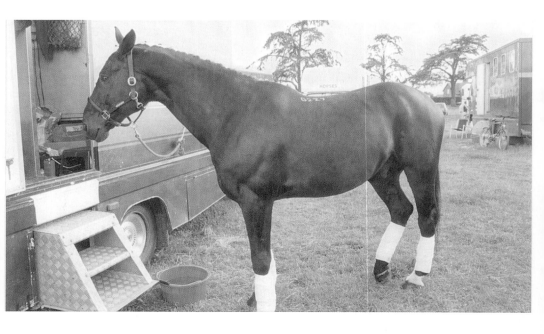

Tied up outside the horsebox Eeyore waiting to be plaited or perhaps seeing if there is any loose food around!

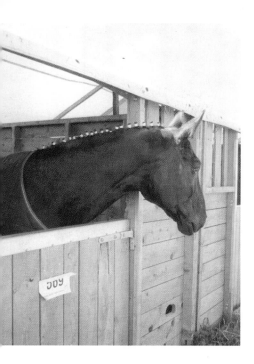

Eeyore again

'My mum was somewhere around here a minute ago!'

'Aha there she is!'

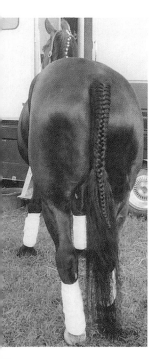

Sophie's famous tail plait

The Pakistan Guide Cavalry and the Indian 61st Cavalry in their stunning costumes parade before the show

Waiting for the Show to begin: a view across the stands and across the Stadium

Smart Uniforms are the order of the day

Excitement increases as the audience begins to arrive

Part of the Household Cavalry arrive

The Mounted Band

Part of the World War II scene, including those gallant pony club riders!

Mounted Police

The King's Troop showing the guns and the gun carriages pulled by teams of six horses

Part of their 'wheel' formation, where teams forming the rim ride a circle outside three groups of riders portraying spokes and a static team represent the central hub

Night time view from the far end of Windsor Show Ground as we approach the Stadium after riding through Victoria Bridge.

The Princess Royal, Princess Anne, as she arrives in the State Landau: Thursday Evening Performance.

King's Troop at full gallop pulling the gun carriages as part of their spectacular routine

The smoke from the firing of the guns gives the Stadium a mysterious atmosphere

A Stage Coach pulled by a team of four greys

Part of Dressage Group 1 performing shoulder-in across
the top of the arena

Everyone who can joins in for the Finale

The Gold Coach parades around the Stadium at the end of the show
during the Finale pulled by eight Windsor Grey horses

Sunday 19th May everyone
has left:

it is like a ghost town!

Even the horsebox field is deserted:
Frogmore reverts back to its normal quiet state.

We come to the line, I sit up, strengthening my stomach and back muscles, keeping my legs around Eeyore's sides and my hands firm but gentle on the reins and he stops, squarely, level on all four legs and stands perfectly still. It is just the best night ever.

We salute as Jennie on Humbug takes a step forward and salutes, and then the applause. Every night it becomes more overpowering. This praise is for everyone in the Balmoral Act, the Side-saddle group, the Scottish dancers, the lady who plays the violin superbly, the parade of Highland and Moorland horses and ponies, the carriages, everyone in the Stadium. Also the music, the orchestra play such a haunting melody that it captures the hearts of everyone who watches.

After our salute, we ride forwards and turn left to be with our partners. Ros whispers to me, 'Hang back a bit, I want to do an extended trot out of the stadium.'

I smile, I am all for that, Eeyore can do the most stunning extended trot, pointing his toes and stretching his legs. He loves to show off.

I half-halt Eeyore, using my stomach and back muscles momentarily to restrain him for a few seconds, almost bringing him to walk, then I ask him to move on again. I do not even have to use the leg aid, just gently take my knees from the saddle a mere centimetre and relax my back. He takes that as a signal and stretches his forelegs out at full length. It is amazing to watch, even more amazing to sit on. I feel as if I am being carried away by Pegasus, up into the air. It makes me smile with joy to be sitting on such an incredible being who uses his power to transport me to a place beyond delight.

Ping, ping, ping, bounce, bounce, bounce. I really know I have a horse and a half beneath me tonight. Both Hooly and Eeyore spring forward, pointing their toes, looking like prima ballerinas. Ros and I laugh with joy.

Directly before we reach the exit is a tent used as a Member's Enclosure. The space in front of the tent, between it and the barrier to the Stadium, is packed tight with row upon row of people. This crowd erupts, applauding and cheering so loudly it is deafening. What a night!

As we part outside the Stadium, my partner going to her left to wait for the Finale and I to the right to hack home, she raises a hand and I do the same; we clap them together, 'Yeah!' She is beaming; I think she has enjoyed her ride too.

Not that everything went according to plan for the rest of the ride. Indeed tonight, there is one of the worst catastrophes ever; a catastrophe that changes the leading file for the big night, Saturday.

We ride the first centre line and the shoulder-in that follows down the long side of the school without mishap. The second time we ride the centre line, it happens. Suddenly, as if from nowhere, a galloping horse streaks across the arena smashing into the leading pair of horses. It occurs so quickly; everyone is stunned for a second or two.

The horse cannons into the chestnuts and both horses are sent reeling to the right from the impact. The riders try to recover their position but one of the chestnuts rears up and refuses to go forward. At which point, the two riders on the greys in second place, thinking quickly, move forward to take over the lead and keep the ride going.

The two chestnuts follow on with Hooly and Eeyore behind them. Fortunately, tonight we left sufficient room behind the pair in front (actually to show off!) and it worked in our favour. We were not affected at all by the crash.

The horse that bolted into the leaders was a bay horse, one of the back pair. The rider was never able to regain complete control. The horse sped around the arena, despite the rider's best efforts.

At one point as Eeyore and I were cantering our first circle I saw her there directly in front of me, the horse was backing up, threatening to rear. There was, fortunately, sufficient room to swerve around and avoid her, but my heart went out to her. I know exactly how she was feeling.

Halfway through the routine, the rider decided to take the horse out of the Stadium before the end of the Act. What had caused the horse to bolt in the first place was a mystery. There were rumours of course! One was that one of the horses in front of the back pair, stopped, reversed and smashed into the horse sending it in panic across the school. There was even a rumour as to which horse it was, but as there is no proof it remains just a rumour. What happens, happens, horses are instinctive creatures, acting spontaneously on impulse.

Sometimes there is no warning, no twitching of the ears, no stiffening of the back muscles. One second everything is relaxed and then for no apparent reason, ping, the horse is two or three yards away from the spot he last filled. His head is in the air, his eyes out on stalks and his whole body is a mass of writhing nerves, of bunched muscles ready for flight. In a situation like 'All the Queens Horses' this is a nightmare. If it happens in a dressage test, or in a private demonstration, then you have the chance to kick on and firmly tell the horse to get on with it.

In a Stadium filled with horses, with Scottish dancers, lights, sounds and the solid mass of an audience, having a horse panic is the nightmare you dread, the depth of horror. I was so relieved that I was not part of it and that Eeyore and I were, at last, able to have a perfectly wonderful ride.

Later back at Frogmore, with Eeyore tucked up for the night, Helena, Sophie and I have a little celebration in the horsebox. Sophie and Helena watched from the side tonight and saw the action on the two huge screens at the back of the Stadium. They state with pride that most of the time the screen shots showed Eeyore and Hooly! Wish I had seen it!

17

Saturday 18th May
Day 7

More drop out – the last performance – The Queen

Here it is, the last day. Time is the strangest phenomena; this week has seemed like years yet it has gone so quickly.

Woke again at 7 a.m., full of delight. What a truly magnificent night! Tonight however is THE ONE, the Queen, this is it, this is what we came for, this is what all the practising, rehearsing, grumbling, groaning, aching, moaning, weariness and despair has been heading towards.

To ride in front of our Queen, yes!!!!! It looks as though I will do it, despite all the pits of despair, heartache and a broken toe that is still extremely sore. (Even weeks later, that toe still hurts whenever it touches the stirrup!)

All this negative emotion disappears into obscurity when we consider that tonight we will ride in front of the Queen. It is the greatest honour of my life to date, and could well be the high point of my career with horses. I am so proud of Eeyore or 'Mr. E' as he is sometimes called down at our livery yard.

Ever since I bought him he has given me so much, taught me incredible amounts about horsemanship, not just riding but being with horses too. As have all the horses and ponies I have owned.

There is nothing so beautiful, honest, giving, loving, courageous, mischievous and as exciting as a horse. A horse can give you the feeling of your spirit soaring, make you laugh with joy and then just as you think you are getting to know them, bump, they bring you right down to earth, literally sometimes!

It is difficult to explain in words why horses evoke such feelings. Perhaps it is because they give so much love.

I treasure those beautiful and precious times with Eeyore; even thinking about them gives me a lump in my throat. As I walk up to his stable he will put his head over the door, he hears my footsteps or perhaps smells my scent. He faces me full on, watching my every move, then he whinnies to me, the loose skin above his nostrils vibrates with the sound.

'Come on Mum, quickly. I have missed you.'

I know I am needed, wanted; he has been waiting for me all morning.

I stroke his forehead and whisper to him. His eyes follow my every movement as if to soak in every memory, savour every instant. Horses live for the moment, they exist only in the now, experiencing to the full every emotion, thought and need that happens each microsecond of life. Not like we who live in the past and future. What will we do tonight, what to eat for tea, what about next week? What did that person say last week? We live so much in the then and maybe that we have little time to live and love in the now.

As I open the door and enter Eeyore's stable, like a true gentleman he steps back to allow me room. He allows me into his space, his 'living room'.

Then with his soft muzzle, he frisks me, nudging me gently, lightly sniffing around my pockets. I know he is looking for titbits, but there is something more, it is an intimate touch between two living creatures, born of a deep, trusting friendship.

I stroke his soft coat, black and shiny, feel his warm muscles rippling underneath. He bends his head around me in his most endearing pose, and how he knows it!

When I ride him he offers me so much. There are times when he transports me out of this world. He dances with me on his back, holding me softly with his muscles and moving with balance and precision. He points his toes in the extended trot, he stretches across and skims the surface in lateral work, he skips divinely in the flying changes.

He is no angel though and there are times when he has his little 'Eeyore' tantrums. If he does not want to work, or do a particular movement, if he thinks he has had enough for today then back go his ears, taut and tight. He kicks out gently with one back leg, he swishes his tail and so clearly do I feel these acts of defiance.

Yes, he does have his 'Eeyore' moods, when he will not comply or submit to doing his work.

At times too he will test me to see if I am still in control, still his head of herd. He will 'pretend' to spook at something, suddenly shooting sideways halfway across the school from where we were. I cannot allow half a ton of horse to control me, because that would be anarchy and extremely dangerous.

So I need to be dominant without being domineering, there is a fine balance between control and tyranny.

From this comes respect for both parties; for a horse needs to respect his rider, just as much as the rider needs to respect the horse. It is a two-way emotion; you need to respect your horse so that he can respect you.

There will always be times when things go wrong, that is the nature of horses and perhaps, too, that is their appeal. There will always be a challenge, especially with a highly bred, highly intelligent, highly trained horse like Eeyore.

My challenge is to earn Eeyore's trust and respect. This can be a more difficult task on an older horse who has already formed his character and 'way of being'. This is one reason why many people buy younger horses whose natures are still pliable; there is more chance of teaching them submission and compliance. Though it is a common mistake that beginner riders, those novice and inexperienced with horses, often buy a young horse 'so that we can learn together.' This is one of the biggest mistakes ever made. It takes an experienced horseperson to teach a young horse, just as it takes an experienced horse or pony to teach a beginner rider.

Not that experience means a constant smooth road, Eeyore still challenges me and there is no doubt that he will go on teaching me about himself and about myself for years to come.

There are those hard times when things go wrong and I cry with complete despair. When the relationship seems impossible and I am close to giving up the challenge. At those times being able to let go would be a blessed release, being able to give up riding and take up some quieter, safer obsession would be sensible. Yet something somewhere deep inside me refuses to capitulate and I know I must continue no matter how difficult the task. When Eeyore and I emerge from those times we often seem to have a deeper and closer relationship.

Eeyore and I have already come a long way together. When I bought him he used to panic at the slightest thing. He does not do this as much now, he is gaining confidence in himself.

There are still occasions when I ask him to do a movement and for an instant I can feel his body tense, feel the panic in his mind. At that point I have to be my most diplomatic. For I have to encourage without bullying; I have to increase his self-confidence without losing the discipline.

The important point is to know the horse, really know and understand his moods, his body language. I can feel a tense muscle; can tell by a twitch of an ear, or a shake of his head what he is feeling. When a rider and horse are that close, when you know what emotions he is experiencing, the relationship becomes ethereal and unique. It is a partnership built on the deepest possible love and respect.

It is perhaps easier with horses than with humans, for horses are genuine creatures, they do not lie; they do not try to deceive. They tell you directly how they are feeling, what they are thinking. There is no dissemblance with horses, their body language is clear.

When their ears are forward it indicates pleasure and joy, ears pricked means excitement; ears erect and pointing means wariness, ready to spook. Ears drooping to the side is relaxation; ears static and flopping means lethargy through sickness or stress. Ears back means watch it, I do not like what you are doing, you are in a 'no no' area. Ears flat back, head turned round, eyes glaring, that's enough, get away or I will bite you. Lips curled, teeth showing, get lost, keep well away. A hind leg raised is a warning; keep away, I may kick. Swinging bottom, leave me alone. Nostrils flared, eyes out on stalks, danger, possible flight. Arched neck, tail out; this looks extremely interesting. Eyes soft, muzzle soft, ears pricked, head towards you, 'I would really love it should you have an apple or sugar lump for me.'

It takes time, usually years, to know a horse, to understand how he is feeling and to be able to coax the best out of him through love, respect and control. Then that moment arrives when everything works, when horse and rider are as one being. That is the greatest feeling in the world!

When the relationship is such that a rider literally thinks and the horse reacts, when two living beings become one, then it is paradise. It may only happen now and again, perhaps that is what makes horse riding an obsession; we are always chasing after that second or two when we are transported to heaven.

This is exactly how I feel today, Saturday, because last night I experienced one of those times with Eeyore.

This morning there will be another autopsy to discuss the happenings of last night. The rumourmongers are busy as the excitement and anticipation heightens. Someone states that there is a meeting at the Catering Tent at 09.00 a.m. I wake up my two neighbouring riders in their horseboxes so that they do not miss the meeting.

By 9.15 it is obvious there is no meeting. It would be interesting to discover who starts these rumours. I see my new partner Ros in the tent and I thank her again for last night. We are still reliving it.

Another rumour is that there is a mounted practice on grass at 2 p.m. Even I think this is illogical. We have one more night to go and, as it has rained overnight, the grass is slippery; to risk horses slipping and going lame now would be suicidal. Jennie Loriston-Clarke is competing today and as she left for Windsor bright and early there is no-one to ask about the rumours.

2 p.m., comes and goes, and there is no practice. I decide to ride Eeyore at 4 p.m., but it takes Sophie two hours to plait his mane. Instead of the large plaits, I request those very small plaits, about thirty of them! Sophie does them beautifully. Then she does his tail plait again.

We did leave the mane and tail plaits in overnight on Wednesday and Thursday and they remained neat and tidy. Sophie though wants Eeyore to be perfect for tonight so she is plaiting the tail again.

By the time she finishes, it is after 5 p.m. We decide to put Eeyore in his stable for tea whilst we prepare for the night.

First though we do his 'exercises' as usual, this is a daily routine. I take a sugar lump, or two, stand by his hindquarters on one side and encourage him to bring his head right round to me for the titbit. Then I repeat this on his other side.

When I first bought him he was so stiff through the neck he could not bend. Now with a little persuasion he will bend his head and neck right around to his flanks. This really helps him to keep his neck and back supple. I can even hear the click-click of his vertebrae sometimes. Another of his exercises is when I place my hand, with sugar lump, between his front legs and near the ground. Here he has to stretch his neck forward and down to retrieve the titbit.

Then I take each foreleg in turn and gently stretch the leg out in front and slightly upwards, but very slowly and gently, this stretches the muscles, ligaments and tendons in the leg and through his torso.

Naturally it helps if I too do daily exercises. I am always determined to do this, and always start off with good intentions....! Time though has that habit of passing; I wish I could put the handbrake to stop time now and then!

18

Saturday 18th May
Day 7 The Evening

Simply the best!

At 6p.m., there is an announcement that all participants should go to the Stable Manager's Office. What now? Another practice? Another autopsy? I sigh heavily; we only have one more night.

As Helena is helping us by riding her bike up and down the field, carrying and fetching stuff for us, and checking on Eeyore, I ask her to see what is happening. She returns and states that I am definitely needed at the Stable Manager's office. So leaving Sophie and Helena to look after Eeyore I walk down to the wooden shed that serves as the Stable Manager's office.

Adjacent to the shed is a gentleman, the same man who organises our Dressage Group as we depart every evening. He is handing out something to various riders. He asks my name, looks down his list, ticks my name off and hands me a square piece of card.

I open the card to discover a photograph inside. It is a lovely picture of the Queen with two skewbald horses. On the flap it states:

'With grateful thanks

for participating in

Her Majesty the Queen's Golden Jubilee.'

What a wonderful gift to receive, fancy Her thinking of us like that!

There is also a book, which every participant is asked to sign, apparently for the Queen to look at and keep. I sign my name under the Dressage section.

Later, I did return to the Office and signed for Eeyore. I thought as he has done a lot of the work he has a right to be in the book. So I wrote on his behalf.

Eeyore //
It has been an honour Your Majesty.
P.S. I love your grass!

The lady working behind the desk seemed to think that the Queen would be amused at that. I wonder if she has ever read it? I would like to think so!

I have to say that I am amazed at Her Majesty's stamina, she is now in her mid seventies and the amount of travelling she has done this year would knock me on my back. Yet she looks as

Canadian Mounties

The Royal Canadian Mounted Police, or RCMP as they are known in these days of initials, were formed by Sir John Macdonald, Canada's first Prime Minister in 1873. Known then as the North Western Mounted Police they brought law, order and Canadian authority to the North West Territories of Alberta and Saskatchewan. They also helped immigrants to settle, fighting diseases, destitution and prairie fires.

In 1904 King Edward VII of England gave them the royal prefix so that they became the Royal North West Mounted Police. During World War 1 they were part of the cavalry divisions sent to France, Belgium and Siberia.

In 1920 they were re-organised to include the Dominion Police. The Royal Canadian Mounted Police came into existence with responsibility for law and order over all of Canada with their distinctive red coated uniforms and Stetson hats.

And those bright red uniforms? These are inherited from the British. The British built a reputation throughout Canada and the 'First Nations People' as being fair minded and respectful. Many of the officers in the early years of RCMP were of British military background and brought with them many British traditions including the uniform similarities.

When the North West Mounted Police marched west in 1873, they dressed in the red tunics so that they could be identified with their British predecessors and easily distinguished from the Americans who wore blue uniforms. Being easily recognised as of British descent in the bright red tunics gave them the confidence and respect of the First Nations. I think this is something we British need to be proud of; British influence throughout the world did have a positive side to it. We are a people of great tolerance and fair mindedness. Perhaps we need to focus on our good points, the positive side of our Empire rather than always picking out the negative areas!

The Stetson hat, made of brown felt, derives from a hat similar to that worn by the American Army. Eventually this style of Stetson hat with a stiff brim and a dented peaked crown become a symbol of the RCMP.

All the horses of the RCMP must be black, elegant, 16 to 17 hands high, have good bone and temperament. 'Bone' is the standard by which horses are judged to be good weight carriers. The actual 'bone' is the cannon bone, its circumference measured just below the knee in a foreleg. A good thick, short cannon bone indicates a good weight carrier, around 9 inches circumference of bone is good. Thoroughbred horses for example normally have slender, long cannons and are not considered good weight carriers. They are bred instead for speed. Horses that are called Cobs, usually have short thick cannons and sturdy bodies, they are built for carrying weight.

The horses of the Canadian Mounties also have to be supple and balanced in their flat work, and have the ability to jump. They must be 'people-friendly' and adaptable to travelling, changing environments, stabling and food. Each horse has a regimental number and all foals born in the same year have names beginning with the same letter of the alphabet. This is quite common in many countries as for instance Holland. The RCMP horses undergo extensive training right from their earliest days as foals. Whilst there is a Musical Division of the Mounties who do perform around the world, this Police force is very much a working force for law and order in Canada.

The Household Cavalry

The Life Guards and the Blues and Royals are the two senior regiments of the Household Cavalry. The Blues and Royals were recently formed in 1969 by combining the Royal Horse Guards (the Blues) and the Royal Dragoons (the Royals) whose histories stretch from the 17th century.

The Royal Horse Guards were formed by Oliver Cromwell from parliamentarians in the North East of England in 1650 prior to his second invasion of Scotland. When Charles II came to the throne, he dismissed the Parliamentarian officers, naturally, and replaced them with men of his own choosing, royalists. Wise man!!

After that the Royal Horse Guards fought in various battles including Waterloo. This regiment became a favourite of George IV and was raised to the status of Household Cavalry in 1820 when the Duke of Wellington became its Colonel.

The Royal Dragoons were formed by Charles II in 1661, after he returned to England as King. The name Dragoon comes from the 'dragon' a special type of musket used by mounted infantry. This regiment was again at the battle of Waterloo in 1815 where they captured the French Eagle of 105th infantry. This eagle is now included in their regimental cipher worn on the left sleeve.

The Life Guards were also formed by Charles II when he regained his throne in 1660. Eighty of his Royalist friends who had been in exile with him formed a personal bodyguard. The band of the Life Guards played kettledrums and trumpets as Charles II entered London in triumph on his restoration. This was another regiment present at the battle of Waterloo. They formed part of the front line that saved the British centre when the Household Cavalry made their famous charge again the French Cuirassiers.

There are almost forty musicians in the Life Guards mounted on black horses of at least 16 hands high, except for the drummer who rides the famous and stunning piebald or skewbald of 17 hands or over. The drummer, needing his hands to play his drums, steers this mighty horse by reins attached to his feet.

Members from the Life Guards and the Blues and Royals form the small ceremonial mounted regiment that escorts the Queen on royal occasions.

The Australian Jackeroos

Hold on to your hats for this one. An Australian Jackeroo is an Australian cowboy; and believe it or not, there is also a Jilleroo. These 'cow' persons, starting off as apprentices and being graded as 2nd or 3rd year Jackeroos, work mainly on farms dealing with cattle and sheep. There are also special schools to teach young people the basic skills of being a Jackeroo or Jilleroo.

sprightly and as full of health as a much younger person. Especially when you think of the time she has had the past few months. It gives me the courage and tenacity to continue. The Queen is an inspiration to us all.

We have a little time tonight before the performance; it seems we do our tasks in half the time now. So I persuade Sophie to take some photographs of the other groups as they depart for Windsor.

First on the scene are those amazing Canadian Mounties in their bright red uniforms and Stetson hats. These are followed by the Arabs, represented by members of the Arab Society mounted on pure-bred Arabian horses. There are also some members of the Household Cavalry, it always gives me a thrill to see them riding with those splendid costumes and helmets. Then come the Australian Jackeroos, all dressed in Australian hats and long raincoats, followed by the 'American' cowboys, some of whom apparently are Spanish or Portuguese riders! Next are the Polo ponies and the Showing Group resplendent in their posh coats and hats.

Once Sophie and Helena have finished with Eeyore, he looks beautiful, an absolute picture. He gleams from head to toe, his black coat shines like a dark mirror, his hooves are painted black with hoof oil, his plaits are taped with white insulating tape and his tail is so neat and perfect. We are proud of him.

Derek arrives at 7.30 p.m. He is going to take Helena and Sophie down to the show. I am amazed at how much this occasion has inspired him. Not being horsey, he is not usually enthusiastic about our events or outings with the horses. He does help, driving the horsebox, supporting us at dressage competitions but normally he does this with little interest. This occasion has elated him beyond recognition. He even wanted to buy some more tickets for tonight at seventy-five pounds a seat to watch the show again! There is something special about this occasion that touches the hearts of all who see it.

I mount at 8 p.m., and go to ride around the field for the last time. The Side-saddle group is there already. There is a heightened excitement this evening. Everyone wishes everybody else 'good luck'. It would be horrifying if anything went wrong tonight. Imagine, having to tell everyone, I fell off in front of the Queen. Off with my head!!!!

Besides anxiety, there is also the feeling of pride; we are now riding in the performance of the week. The horses feel it too; they seem full of life and anticipation.

Here are the rest of my group; apart from those we will meet at Windsor. With great joy I am again partnering Ros with her horse Hooly. We meet and pose for some photographers who wish to take pictures of the last night.

Then for the last time we start our forty-five minute ride to Windsor. I must take in everything around me tonight; I will probably never pass this way again. We ride out of the field down the dusty path along the old brick wall that marks the boundary of lovely Frogmore House.

There is a tent at the end of this lane, outside of which two soldiers wave at us and wish us luck. Everyone is so cheerful tonight; there is a feeling of companionship, of belonging. There are several soldiers along our route, I wonder if they will manage to see or meet the Queen. It makes a difference having them all along the route, makes us feel safe.

I ride next to my partner along the bush lined path and off to our right, straight across at the crossroads and follow the track down by the fields where the cows are grazing. Turn left then right, walk down the long path past the heron field. Rhododendron bushes, thick and oily green, screen the path to our left; we make our way down to a bridge and along the grass verge where the guns go off!

Boom, boom, boom, boom-boom-boom. There they go and still some of the horses scatter around and pretend to be frightened. They have to keep their riders on their toes somehow.

Under Victoria Bridge, which the horses do not even notice, up the rise to the left past the now waiting Side-saddle Group. They all wish us good luck and we return their greeting.

There are crowds and crowds of people everywhere. Each night has been progressively busier but tonight there are people all along the roadside and to our right along the fence. The place is buzzing. The car park is packed.

People begin to cheer and wish us luck; they wave flags and streamers at us. We feel like royalty ourselves with all this adoration. I also feel a little sickness inside my stomach; this is it, the big night. Eeyore walks along quietly and calmly, his ears relaxed, he takes the applause as normal, and totally warranted for such a wonderful horse.

We walk through the caravan park towards the collecting ring; people line up three and four deep. Faces, faces everywhere, voices cheering and crying out to us. I never thought to experience anything like this in my life. Even the noise from the Stadium seems ten times louder tonight and the lights brighter, or is that my imagination?

In the collecting ring we start to warm up, trotting in our pairs around in circles. There is a change of leaders tonight; the two grey horses are now in front followed by the two chestnuts, then Hooly and Eeyore. This decision must have been made earlier today.

We begin to canter, first in a circle then a figure of eight with a flying change in the centre. The pace seems a little fast so we ask the leaders to slow down a fraction. It must be nerve-wracking for them, being leaders for the first time on the last night! The pace slows and that works much better.

A man starts to wave us in, he states loudly that the Dressage Group need to move through to the now familiar Chute. Here we wait once more, surrounded by crowds.

To our left the road above us is crowded with people, three and four rows thick. The sound emanating from them is like the murmuring of waves on a shore. To our right is another crowd. Lines of people, ten deep, wait here. Shadowy faces watching us, interested and expectant, their anticipation like a halted breath steals the silence around us.

As Hooly and Eeyore wait side by side, the sounds of the Act before ours echo through the narrow channel. The greys become a little edgy, they are in front for the first time; they move about from side to side. Riders shush their horses, cooing like doves, trying to defuse the excitement that may turn into restlessness and speed.

The lone piper starts and the Group moves forward.

As we trot in, the crowd to our right go mad, cheering, yelling, clapping, stamping. Though they are no more than a crush of pale faces, we can feel their presence and excitement.

If we thought that the previous night's noise was a tidal wave, the applause that greets us now is a positive tsunami. It hits us like a force field.

The spotlights guide our path, shining into our faces so that the audience in front is a black mass sparked by intermittent blue starred camera flashes.

There, yes, there right in the middle is the Queen sitting with Prince Philip and Prince Andrew. Should I turn to my right and bow? Wish I had asked if that was OK. I watch those in front but they ride on ahead, so I do the same though the temptation to peek is almost too overpowering.

Eeyore extends his trot as he bounds on, lifting himself up and moving beautifully, he feels really on his toes but relaxed, I do believe he is enjoying himself.

In one of those strange twists of time, our routine seems to go slower tonight as if held in a time warp. Strange, when we first performed this drill it seemed to go so fast. Tonight, though we do nothing different, each step seems to be suspended. There is even time to look around the stadium.

The two great screens at the back, one either side of the proscenium, show snatches of the scene below. The Scottish dancers are reeling and whirling in their tartans, performing in full spotlight. I see the RDA, the Riding for the Disabled, parade past our arena. The riders are dressed in blue outfits and their horses are led by volunteers.

Following is a line of Mountain and Moorland ponies. These gallant animals are stunning to look at with their long flowing manes and tails like wedding veils. There are carriages and carts pulled by horses and ponies, and tiny Shetland ponies led in hand.

I can even see a glimpse of the Side-saddle group performing their drill at the back. The lights, the smells, the sounds, I want to take in every microsecond; I want to commit this to my memory forever.

Especially as Eeyore performs like an angel; he transports me on his ebony wings. It is like a dream. Being able to ride a horse like Eeyore in such a unique occasion is a dream made real. I am beaming with delight; I love it.

He floats; I swear his feet do not touch the ground. As he moves it is as if I am sitting on a cloud suspended above the earth. He holds his head, carrying his body so that I feel the lightest touch in my hands through the reins to the bit in his soft, warm, moist mouth. He responds to the lightest movement of my leg turning with ease and fluency. He pricks his ears as the applause reaches a rhythmical height in time to the music. The crowd is going wild and Eeyore is lapping it up.

The circles are perfect; the half-passes flow in unison and the canter work is perfection. Secretly I hope they will ask for a encore!!!! I do so want to do it all again and again.

All too soon, it is over. We shoulder-in along the top side and down to the centre line where we stand. This time I make Eeyore stand still by keeping my leg on and my hands firm. I have learnt such a lot from doing this, in many, many ways.

Now we wait for the GP riders who are coming down their centre line at passage. We salute and accept the acclaim. The applause is deafening, crashing into us like a solid wave.

We did it, we did it; Eeyore and I did it. We rode in front of the Queen!

As we exit with our group, Ros and I hold back to go for another extended trot. The horses are so lit up tonight though that they go straight into collected canter. So what? We did it. We rode in front of our Queen and did not disgrace ourselves.

Derek, Sophie and Helena meet us on the track from the Stadium. They are full of congratulations and praise. They are shouting, 'Well done, well done, that was brilliant.'

Hundreds of people are lining this road tonight, cheering us; it is like being on parade. This must be how the Queen feels when everyone cheers for her. What a feeling!! It is adrenalin-boosting, fills me with pride and is probably addictive. The emotions catch me just at the top of my stomach, traditionally supposed to be the seat of feeling. I can feel a sting in my eyes and a salt taste on my tongue. It is almost too much, almost!

Derek is speaking to me as I ride along, but at first I can hear nothing. Then as my head clears I listen carefully. He says that I can be in the Finale on foot should I so wish it.

'What about Eeyore?' I ask.

'Sophie can ride Eeyore home,' he suggests.

'OK' I answer. It would be good for Sophie to ride Eeyore back, she would get a 'feel' of that hack from horseback instead of on a cycle. So I stop, dismount and prepare to give her a leg up.

I am surprised as I hold her leg; she is shaking all through. She is literally shivering like a jelly.

'I'm so nervous,' she whispers as we alter her stirrups. 'I don't know the way back.'

With great kindness, one of the GP riders stops and turns around, 'I will ride with her,' she says. Thank you so much.

I watch as they ride off together and hope that Sophie will enjoy it. She will; she loves Eeyore and he will look after her.

We make our way back to the show, walking around the outside of the Stadium. Unfortunately, we cannot manage to find an entrance point to the show. No matter which area we try, we keep being stopped by army personnel. They politely inform us to make our way around to the other side.

Suddenly I feel tired and, though I know Derek is eager for me to be a part of the Finale, I realise I do not want it. I know this sounds odd, but I feel as though something is missing, something vital like an arm or a leg. I do not want to be in it, not without Eeyore.

We did it together, without him it would not feel right. Trying to explain this to Derek is difficult, I am not sure he understands, but as I look at my youngest daughter Helena, she nods in agreement.

I also want to be back at the stable ready for when Sophie arrives. Every night that I have hacked back, it has been so comforting to find someone waiting there. We leave the Finale and drive back to Frogmore. I am happy with that.

Arriving at Frogmore before Sophie we are able to prepare Eeyore's stable, skip it out, clean and refill the water buckets, put fresh hay in the haynet and make a small midnight feed.

Then we wait. It is fortunate that we returned early, the traffic around Windsor after the show is horrendous. Vehicles wait up to an hour to exit the car parks.

We hear the clip clop of hooves along the dusty lane. Then Sophie comes into the light. She is looking relaxed now; she has that 'Eeyore' beam on her face.

As she dismounts, she relates to us her adventure along the hack. She really enjoyed it, how different the ride is on horseback in the dark. At one point, her and the GP rider trotted to catch some others up, and Eeyore did his huge springy trot. The GP rider looked on with amazement and said 'Wow Eeyore you have got a huge trot there.' Sophie beams with pride. Eeyore is certainly the horse you can show off on!

After a moment's silence the GP rider turns to Sophie and queries, 'You said his name is Eeyore II?' Sophie sighs; she knows what is coming.

'I know him,' states the GP rider as her face lights up. 'He's famous.'

Derek and Helena decide to go home, they both look very tired. It has been a long week for us all and now that it is almost finished the weariness begins to take effect. Sophie and I have planned to go to the last night party that starts at 12.30 a.m. We have been looking forward to this 'do' all week. Apparently it is going to be quite wild!

I look at my watch, it is only just gone 11, so as it is too early we walk to the horsebox for a drink and a rest.

I guess we were too tired. By the time 12.30 came and the party started, I am afraid to admit that both Sophie and I are fast asleep!

I did hear later that the party lived up to its name, with people swinging from the tent poles. It was organised sublimely and I can only apologise most profusely that I missed it. It was the biggest disappointment of the week!!!!

19

Sunday 19th May
The Last Day

We say goodbye – shop and depart

It is so, so sad when something like this ends. It is highly unlikely that there will be another occasion of this magnitude again in our lifetime. It is even more unlikely that I and Eeyore will be part of anything this stupendous or memorable. There were moments when I wished I had not started it but now I wish it would never end.

Sunday is a glorious summer day, the sun is shining, there is a gentle breeze and life goes on. Odd, there are times when you think life should stop. The death of a loved one, the birth of a child, an event like this, you feel everything should stop. It feels as though the whole world should take some time out to ponder, should stop to share with you this point in your life. Life however, goes on inexorably, 'the moving finger writes and having writ moves on'. The wheel revolves unemotionally, uncaring, unaware of anything that happens.

Sophie and I are living a day of contrasts, elation mixed with depression, activity and lethargy, aching muscles and bones, but bodies full of energy and life. I desperately need to rest, as does Eeyore and Sophie, but I am reluctant to leave Frogmore and Windsor. Once we go, the spell will be broken; the dream will dissipate with the passage of time.

Slowly as people leave Frogmore, more and more stables become empty. The whole complex transforms into a ghost town; people and horses leave only their memory. The stable door creaks in the breeze, old hay and straw blow along in the dust, the canvas roof flaps but no horses hear it.

As I walk around the empty field, it is desolate and sad. The only remnants of this week are hoof prints in the dried mud, abandoned bales of hay, flattened patches of grass where horseboxes were parked. There are no neighings, no munchings of grass or hay, no whinnyings, no swish of a tail; it is all so silent, a graveyard of memories.

We visit the Windsor Show Ground once more where people are still shopping and riders are still jumping those seemingly impossibly high fences; visitors are eating their meals. It is so normal; I feel like shouting out, 'I have ridden in front of the Queen.' Everyone should know.

I feel apart from everyone else, as though I am in a different point in time. I have experienced something they will not. I am out of step with the human race, phased into a different dimension. I shiver at these thoughts that pass through my mind.

As I look around at the normal people here, I realise that their lives do not touch mine and neither does mine touch theirs.

Perhaps that is untrue. If I wrote about this experience, explaining and describing the emotions, the trials and tribulations of that week, perhaps then I could share this great honour with someone.

The whole week has been a revelation. I have learnt so much about myself, about my horse and about my dear daughters Sophie and Helena. I have been particularly surprised about Martyn my son and Derek; I cannot believe that they have shown such emotion. Above all I did my own small part in celebrating the Queen's Golden Jubilee, it was a special honour to be able to perform in front of the Queen and the Royal Family.

'All the Queen's Horses' worked on so many levels, personally, individually, collectively, emotionally, physically, mentally and spiritually. I hope that by sharing this experience I will, in some part, be able to keep this remarkable week alive, keep the feelings fresh in the memories of those who participated and for those who watched the performances. I would like to pay tribute to all those riders, grooms and supporters, their horses and ponies who took part.

By describing this eventful week I would also like to create in those who were not present a taste of the magic we experienced when participating in such an occasion. Perhaps this tale will encourage others to reach for the stars and, despite failing time after time, to endure until through determination, perseverance and the friendship of horse and human, they too will succeed in fulfilling their life's dream.

I hope I have been able to explain the absolute beauty of horses, the bond that grows between a horse and his human. I would like to describe how there is nothing on earth like this relationship.

Most of all I would like to express the love I bear for Eeyore, the privilege and honour it is to ride him and how so, so fortunate I am to know a horse as wonderful, generous and loving as he. My tribute is to him, Eeyore II.

'Never mind the praise, Mum, just give me the sugar lumps.'
Eeyore has the last word.

Synopsis of
'All the Queen's Horses'

The Acts and the Timetable

Show begins 9 p.m. duration approximately 90 minutes

ARRIVAL

- The arrival with mounted Police escorting a Landau from the Royal Mews
- Followed by the Household Cavalry's escort and the Mounted Band
- Fanfare of trumpets by the Irish Guards
- The Choir consists of 15 choristers from St. George's Chapel Choir and another 117 from the Windsor & Eton Choral Society

ACT ONE – The Beginning

- Re-enactment of scenes from World War II with various heavy horse drawn vehicles, drays, carts, carriages. Market and Refuse Carts, Coal, Farriers and Brewery Drays. Light horse vehicles include Butchers and Costermongers carts, Post Office van and Delivery Brougham
- Entrance of pit ponies
- Children and adults dressed in 1940's clothing take part in an air raid, lights flashing, drums sounding like Ack Ack fire.

ACT TWO – Renaming of Kings Troop

- The King's Troop enter in procession
- Re-enactment of the renaming of the Royal Horse Artillery as the King's Troop by George VI, Queen Elizabeth's father
- Kings troop with artillery galloping across arena in various movements. Guns salute

ACT THREE – Foreign and Commonwealth

- Entrance of representatives of the commonwealth and foreign countries where the Queen has made visits
- The Royal Canadian Mounted Police
- North African Arabs
- Australian Jackeroos

- Indian Cavalry
- Mounted unit from the Pakistani cavalry
- American coach and team
- American Cowboys
- Appaloosas
- American Servicemen
- French Garde Republicaine
- Kenyan mounted police
- Pony Club members carrying Commonwealth flags

ACT FOUR – Racing and Hunting

- Shetland pony Grand National. Enactment of the Grand National Race with Shetland Ponies together with bookies and commentator. Gallant little ponies set off from the starting post and gallop as fast as their little crooked legs will take them around an oval 'race track'
- Racing also represented by Point to Point horses and racehorses. Included are some of her Majesty's racehorses and jockeys in the Queen's colours and those of the Royal Family
- On the last night, Saturday, a special guest appearance was given by Desert Orchid, that amazing racehorse. He paraded around bright eyed with his grey ears pricked, playing to the crowd. He loved it, lapping up the applause; in fact he did not want to leave the stadium!
- Also in this scene are representatives of the hunting fraternity together with hounds

ACT FIVE – Polo, Polo Cross and Horse Ball

- The game of Polo is explained. This game is reputed to have originated with Mongolian horsemen who used to cut off the heads of their enemies and then knock them around from horseback. Gallant members of the Pony club dressed in 'Mongolian' costumes demonstrated this skill, thankfully not with a real head!
- The new sport of 'Horse Ball' was represented in this Act

ACT SIX – Carriages and Carts

- All types, sizes and ages of carriages are represented, singles, pairs and teams. Grand and 'not so grand' carriages and Passenger carriages
- Shetland pony carts
- Gigs and Scurry carts drawn by Hackneys and Welsh ponies
- Phaetons, Norfolk carts, Dog Carts, Village Cart and Queen Victoria's Carriage
- Coaches and teams

ACT SEVEN -Balmoral Scene

- Entrance of dressage riders to lone piper
- Highland dancers with lady violinist

- Intermediate riders, Grand Prix riders and a group representing the Side Saddle Association
- Parading through this scene are Highland and Moorland Ponies and Cobs, Riding for the Disabled, Carriages and Carts
- Music accompaniment Lone Piper, Scottish Reel and 'The Gael' from the Last of the Mohicans

ACT EIGHT - Dream Sequence

- One incredible Grey-white horse, Pegasus, with lady rider 'flying'
- Coloured horse carousel, coloured horses with riders in beautiful costumes riding around a 'maypole'
- Circus horses and high school horses performing movements such as vaulting, passage and piaffes

ACT NINE – Pony Club

- Gallant members of the Pony Club doing gymkhana events. Vaulting on and off ponies at gallop. Amazing feats of riding and courage. These riders must go down as one of the most gallant and talented in the evening

ACT TEN – Parade of the Queen's Horses

- Representatives of the horses and carriages owned by Her Majesty the Queen
- The King's Troop
- The Household Cavalry
- The HC Drum Horse
- The Royal Scots Dragoon Guards and Drum Horse
- Argyll and Sutherland Highlanders Mascot
- Household Cavalry Mounted Band

ACT ELEVEN – Household Cavalry and Mounted Police

- Household Cavalry perform a drill ride with two of the horses lying down in the centre.
- Police demonstrate their amazing skills by jumping over small brush fences, first in a figure of eight. Then they take off their jackets, then take away their stirrups removing them completely from the saddles. They proceed to undo their girths and remove their saddles, at canter over fences!

FINALE – All participants

- Entrance of representatives of all the acts, the horses, riders and performers together with the HC Mounted Band, the Fanfare of trumpeters by the Irish Guards, Drum horses and Captain's Escort
- Gold State Coach to be pulled by eight Windsor Grey Horses around the Stadium escorted by walking grooms, Postillions, Footmen and Yeomen of the Guard
- Music accompaniment Zadok the Priest by Handel
- A Single Perfect White Horse to rear as the End